What is
Proportional Representation?

What is
Proportional Representation?

A guide to the issues

VERNON BOGDANOR

Martin Robertson

© Vernon Bogdanor, 1984

First published in 1984 by Martin Robertson &
Company Ltd., 108 Cowley Road, Oxford OX4 1JF.

British Library Cataloguing in Publication Data

Bogdanor, Vernon
    What is proportional representation?
    1. Proportional representation – Great Britain
    I. Title
    324.6'3   J1075.G7

    ISBN 0–85520–740–X
    ISBN 0–85520–741–8   Pbk

Typeset by The Spartan Press Ltd, Lymington, Hants
Printed and bound in Great Britain by
Billing and Sons Ltd, Worcester

For Judy, Paul and Adam,
disproportionately

Contents

Preface   ix

1   Introduction   1

2   The British Electoral System   14

3   The Alternative Vote and the Two-Ballot System   30

4   Proportional Representation: The German System   46

5   Proportional Representation: The Single Transferable Vote   75

6   Women and Ethnic Minorities   111

7   Some Consequences of Proportional Representation   127

8   Proportional Representation and the Condition of Britain   142

Suggestions for Further Reading   158

Index   161

Preface

The purpose of this book is to present and evaluate the various methods by which British voters can elect their MPs. How Parliament should be elected is undoubtedly one of the most important issues facing any democrat, and the debate over proportional representation has made it a question of pressing political concern. Yet too much of the debate has taken the form of unsupported generalities, and it is time to be more specific.

Although this book reaches certain definite conclusions, I shall not be too disappointed if readers of *What is Proportional Representation?* emerge with a different verdict. For the book's purpose is to clarify rather than to convert.

I should like to thank those who have helped me in the preparation of this book. Clive Payne of the Oxford University Social Studies Faculty's Computing Unit provided the simulations which appear in chapter 2; while David Butler of Nuffield College, Oxford, Brian Farrell of University College, Dublin, Margit Hosseini of the Federal German Embassy in London, and Mariot Leslie from the British Embassy in Bonn, all gave valuable information in response to my importunate inquiries.

I should also like to thank Ivor Crewe of Essex University for permission to quote from his article 'Electoral Reform and the Local MP' in chapter 5; Ted Nealon of the Department of the Taoiseach, Dublin, for allowing me to use his diagram of the Carlow–Kilkenny constituency in chapter 5; and Brian

Whitt for allowing me to quote from his pamphlet on electoral reform in the same chapter. I want also to thank my college, Brasenose, for its assistance and support.

But, above all, I am deeply grateful to my wife and two sons, Paul and Adam, for tolerating the disproportionate amount of time which I spend on electoral systems. It is to them that this book is dedicated.

Vernon Bogdanor
Oxford, October 1983

1

Introduction

It is in the nature of general elections in Britain that there should be winners and losers, and it is hardly surprising that election results leave the winners elated and the losers dispirited. Yet the losers rarely question the fairness of the result itself. They may, of course, feel that the electorate has not appreciated sufficiently the virtues of their party or the defects of the other side. Nevertheless, the reaction of the losing parties and of those voters who have supported them is generally to reconsider their policies, perhaps to change their leader and then to prepare for the next contest, at which, so they believe, virtue will surely triumph.

The 1983 general election in Britain did not quite follow this pattern, however, for it has given rise to considerable misgivings about whether the result actually reflected the real opinions of the electorate. This anxiety was by no means confined to political opponents of the Government but was also shared by many Conservatives. There is, in Britain, a widely diffused sense of fairness, and no one likes to win any contest – whether electoral or sporting – by methods which cannot be justified as equitable. As a result of the 1983 election, the very electoral process itself has come under challenge; and there is renewed interest in alternative methods of election, and especially in proportional representation. In July 1983, one month after the election, a number of leading politicians, including Sir Ian Gilmour, a former Conservative Cabinet Minister, Roy Jenkins, the first leader of the Social

Democrats, and Austin Mitchell, a prominent Labour MP, together with such non-political figures as Sir Peter Parker, the former chairman of British Rail, and Sir Richard Attenborough, the film director, joined together to sponsor an all-party national petition whose aim is to secure a referendum on whether the British electoral system should be changed. The topic of proportional representation is likely to remain a part of the political agenda for a considerable time to come.

Many people will undoubtedly resent having to consider the issues involved in proportional representation. To them proportional representation is a profoundly boring subject, and many of its supporters seem eccentric or even fanatical disputants about electoral matters in a language imbued with technicalities that cannot easily be understood by the uninitiated. Above all, many cannot understand why it is that so much attention is given to the issue. Is it not an irrelevant distraction from the intractable economic and social problems which Britain has to face? Is it not peripheral to the real issues and remote from the central questions of politics? Cannot proportional representation be left to academics and experts, while the citizens direct their attention to the problem of deciding between the competing philosophies of the parties which seek their votes?

This book has a twofold purpose. The first is to explain in perfectly straightforward terms the issues behind proportional representation, the arguments for changing the British electoral system to a proportional one and the arguments against change. The instincts of those who distrust the technical atmosphere in which proportional representation is usually discussed are, by and large, justified. There is no reason why the issues cannot be explained in everyday language, and there need be no mystery about them. It is not the arguments themselves which are difficult, but rather the weighing up of conflicting considerations to reach a verdict. For the debate over proportional representation, like most political issues perhaps, is not one in which all the good arguments are on one side. There are good arguments on both sides, and two people can easily find themselves reaching different conclusions through weighing up the same arguments differently. The purpose of this book is not to coerce readers into accepting a particular conclusion, but rather to put before them the main considerations upon which any conclusions must be based.

The book also has a second purpose. It is to show that the issue of proportional representation, whatever view is taken of it, is profoundly important for the future of British politics and government. Far from being a mere distraction from the real issues of social and economic policy, it is intimately bound up with them. Indeed, it is not going too far to suggest that the future shape of British politics will be very largely influenced by whether we decide to retain our electoral system or change it to a proportional one. For this reason every voter ought to be as much aware of the arguments about proportional representation as of the philosophies of the main political parties.

The Result of the 1983 General Election in Britain

The best starting point is to look at the result of the 1983 general election, considering not only the number of seats which each party won but also the number of votes each party polled and each party's percentage of the vote.

TABLE 1   *The results of the British general election of 1983*

Party	Seats won	Votes polled	% vote
Conservative	397	13,012,315	42.4
Labour	209	8,456,934	27.6
Liberal/SDP Alliance	23	7,780,949	25.4
Scottish National Party	2	331,975	1.1
Plaid Cymru	2	125,309	0.4
Northern Ireland parties	17	764,925	2.5
Other parties	0	203,589	0.6

The Conservatives won a landslide majority in terms of seats – 188 seats more than Labour and a majority of 144 seats over all other parties. This was the largest overall majority since the war except for Labour's majority of 146 in 1945. Yet, as can be seen from table 1, the Conservatives did not succeed in gaining a majority of the votes cast. Indeed, they gained only a little over 40 per cent – two-fifths of the vote. Mrs Thatcher's Government, therefore, is a majority Government only in terms of enjoying a majority of seats in the Commons. In terms of votes cast her Government is not a majority Government but one representing the largest minority. In this it does not differ from any other post-war British Government, none of which has succeeded in gaining 50 per cent of the vote. So in Britain it would be a mistake to equate democracy with majority government, if by that we mean a Government commanding a majority of the *votes cast* as opposed to *seats won*.

Turning now to the Opposition parties, we see that Labour won 209 out of the 650 seats in the Commons – just over 32 per cent of the seats – for 27.6 per cent of the vote; while the Liberal/SDP Alliance, whose total vote was only 675,985 less than Labour's, secured only 23 of the 650 Commons seats – a mere 3.5 per cent of the seats. The Alliance gained nearly the same vote as Labour, but Labour secured nine times as many seats.

We shall have to look a little more closely at how it is possible, under the British electoral system, for two parties to win almost exactly the same number of votes only to be rewarded with a very different number of seats. What should be already clear is that the Commons, for better or worse, is very far from being an exact mirror of political opinion in the country. The British electoral system, so it seems, rewards some parties while penalizing others.

We can look at the same facts in another way by asking how many votes were needed to elect an MP from each of the main political groupings. If we divide the Conservative vote, 13,012,315, by the number of seats, 397, we find that it took nearly 33,000 votes to elect a Conservative MP. If we perform the same operation with the Labour vote, we find that it took just over 40,000 votes to elect a Labour MP; while it took no fewer than 338,000 votes to elect an MP from the Alliance. It would seem, then, that in terms of the chances of electing an MP a vote for the Conservatives was worth slightly more than a vote for Labour but ten times as much as a vote for the Alliance, while a vote for Labour was worth nearly eight and a half times as much as a vote for the Alliance. Not every vote that is cast in a British general election, therefore, is of equal value; the votes cast for some parties are worth much more than the votes cast for others. Britain enjoys political equality in that every person over 18 not otherwise disqualified has one vote. But it does not have political equality in the sense of every vote having an equal value.

The Conservatives were clearly the major beneficiaries of the discrepancy between votes and seats, but Labour also benefited to some extent, receiving about 30 more seats than it would under a system which allocated seats proportionately according to votes cast. Those voting for one of the two major parties – 70 per cent – found themselves rewarded by the electoral system, since the two major parties gained 606 seats out of the 650 in the Commons – no less than 93 per cent of the seats; while the 30 per cent of those voting who chose to support a party other than the Conservatives or Labour gained only 7 per cent of the seats in the Commons. Visitors to the House of Commons, therefore, would gain the quite erroneous impression that Britain had retained her two-party system. They would see nearly 400 Conservatives crowding the Government benches and over 200 Labour Members dominating the Opposition benches. MPs from the other parties would probably be too few to capture their attention. Unless they were aware of how many votes were cast for each party, they would not appreciate that a minuscule grouping in the Commons – the Alliance with its 23 MPs – actually enjoyed the support of over a quarter of the voters. In parliamentary terms, therefore, Britain remains a two-party system; but in electoral terms, as the figures in table 1 show, there are three political groupings competing for power, any one of which could, in theory, win the general election of 1987 or 1988.

Elections under Proportional Representation

What is clear, then, is that the House of Commons is not a forum within which the seats gained by each party accurately reflect the number of votes cast for them: and, to be fair, none of the defenders of the British electoral system has ever pretended otherwise. Their defence of the system is based not on its ability to produce precisely accurate representation but on its possession of other virtues which, in their opinion, outweigh the value of accurate representation. But before beginning to consider the pros and cons of Britain's electoral system in more detail, let us perform a couple of thought experiments by considering how the same number of votes can produce different outcomes under different electoral systems.

Let us suppose, first, that Britain possessed an electoral system which allocated seats in the Commons in exact proportion to the number of votes cast. In fact, none of the systems of proportional representation yields *exact* proportionality for reasons which will be discussed later (although the electoral systems used in the Netherlands and Israel come the closest to this ideal), and the vast majority of those who want to change Britain's electoral system certainly do not favour a proportional system of such a precise kind. But that need not detract from the value of the thought experiment.

It might be objected that a thought experiment of the kind which we are intending to conduct is of little use for another reason. If Britain had a system of proportional representation, then, it can be argued, voting habits themselves would change. The votes cast in a general election would *not* then be as shown in table 1, since voters might, for example, be tempted to support small parties which, under our present electoral system, stand little chance of returning many MPs but which, under proportional representation, could establish a firm foothold in the Commons.

This objection is, in a sense, perfectly justified. But it is not very helpful, since it is quite impossible to predict precisely how voting patterns would change under an alternative electoral system. Let us, therefore make the simplifying assumption that the votes cast were exactly the same as in the 1983 general election but that the seats were allocated on a perfectly proportional basis. Then, instead of the result of the election being:

Conservatives	397 seats
Labour	209 seats
Alliance	23 seats
SNP	2 seats
Plaid Cymru	2 seats
Northern Ireland parties	17 seats

it would have been:

Conservatives	276 seats
Labour	179 seats
Alliance	165 seats
SNP	7 seats
Plaid Cymru	3 seats
Northern Ireland parties	16 seats
Others	4 seats

If the 1983 general election had been fought under a proportional electoral system, the most obvious consequence would have been that the Conservatives would no longer have an overall majority of seats: they would in fact be 50 seats short of the 326 needed for an overall majority. Further, the number of seats won by the Alliance would have increased sevenfold, so that the Alliance would have only 14 fewer seats than Labour.

This would have had the further consequence that no

majority Government could have been formed after the
(hypothetical) election. Instead, either Britain would have a
minority Government, as it did between February and October 1974, or, if two of the major groupings could agree
upon a programme, there might be a coalition Government
of the kind that ruled Britain during much of the period of
the two world wars and for most of the 1930s. It is not
possible to predict the political colour of the Government
which would have followed such an election, carried out
under a proportional electoral system. The Conservatives, as
by far the largest party, might have carried on ruling as a
minority. If they had done so, they would have had to
ensure that their legislation was such as could gain the
support of enough MPs from outside the Conservative Party
to secure a parliamentary majority. Alternatively, the Conservatives might have formed a coalition with the Alliance
parties (a coalition with Labour would, of course, have been
highly unlikely). In this case also the Conservatives would
have had to ensure that their policies were acceptable to
their coalition partners. But whatever the precise outcome, it
is clear that both the *type of government* and the *legislation
which resulted* would have been very different from the
actual course of events. Whether the hypothetical outcome
would have been better or worse than the actual result is, in
large part, a matter of political predilection, and we shall
return to this issue later in the book. But at least it is clear
that the outcome would have been *different*. The change to
a proportional system of election would have made a fundamental and important impact upon the government of
Britain.

Let us now continue our thought experiment by looking
at the general election before 1983, that of 1979. The 1979
general election was also won by the Conservatives under
Mrs Thatcher, who succeeded in displacing from office
James Callaghan's minority Labour Government. The actual
result of the 1979 general election is shown in table 2.

TABLE 2   *The results of the British general election of 1979*

Party	Seats won	Votes polled	% vote
Conservative	339	13,697,690	43.9
Labour	269	11,532,148	36.9
Liberal	11	4,313,811	13.8
Scottish National Party	2	504,259	1.6
Plaid Cymru	2	132,544	0.4
Northern Ireland parties	12	695,889	2.2
Other parties	0	343,674	1.2

In an election held under a strictly proportional system, assuming that voting patterns remained the same, the result would have been, in terms of seats:

Conservatives	279 seats
Labour	234 seats
Liberal	88 seats
SNP	10 seats
Plaid Cymru	2 seats
Northern Ireland parties	14 seats
Other parties	8 seats

Here also no single party would have enjoyed an overall majority, and the Conservatives, the largest party, would have been 39 seats short of an overall majority. But although the Conservatives were the largest party, it is by no means clear that they would have been able to form a Government, for during much of 1977 and 1978 James Callaghan's minority Labour Government had been sustained by the Liberals under the terms of the 'Lib–Lab pact'. If Callaghan could have succeeded in renewing that pact, he would, with the Liberals, have been able to command a majority in the Commons and could have continued in Government. Little would have been heard of Mrs Thatcher's 'new Conservatism' and less, perhaps, of the Labour Party being in a state of irretrievable decline. British history from 1979 would clearly have taken a very different course; whether for better or worse is again a matter of individual judgement, but it would have been different.

Now, let us perform a final thought experiment, but this time with a general election in another country, the Federal Republic of Germany (West Germany). We shall discuss the German electoral system in detail later on, but for the moment it is sufficient to say that the system gives a result which is exactly proportional, except that any party which fails to win 5 per cent of the vote or three constituency seats is not given any seats at all in the Bundestag (the German lower house, equivalent roughly to our House of Commons). The three main parties in Germany are roughly equivalent to our Conservative, Labour and Liberal parties. They are the Christian Democrats (CDU/CSU), a moderate conservative party; the Social Democrats (SPD), a moderate party of the left; and the Free Democrats (FDP), a liberal party. In the German elections of 1976 and 1980, which we are now going to consider, these were the only parties which succeeded in winning seats in the Bundestag.

Let us first consider the 1976 German election. The percentage of the vote secured by the three main parties was as follows:

CDU/CSU	48.6%
SPD	42.6%
FDP	7.9%

The conservative party, the CDU/CSU, succeeded in gaining 6 per cent more of the vote than its closest rival, the SPD. Its proportion of the vote, 48.6 per cent, was higher than has been achieved by any British Government in an election since the war, except for 1955 and 1959. Neither in 1945, when Labour gained an overall majority of 146, nor in 1983, when, as we have seen, the Conservatives won an overall majority of 144, did British Governments succeed in winning as much as 48.6 per cent of the vote.

It might have been assumed, then, that the German Christian Democrats would form a Government after the elections of 1976. But that, in fact, did not happen. The proportional electoral system in West Germany gave the parties the following number of seats in the Bundestag:

CDU/CSU	243 seats
SPD	214 seats
FDP	39 seats

Out of the 496 seats in the Bundestag, the CDU/CSU were just five short of an overall majority. This was, however, sufficient to keep them out of power. For the SPD Prime Minister, Helmut Schmidt, had been in coalition with the Liberal FDP, and in the election campaign the two parties told voters that they proposed to continue with their coalition after the election. The Free Democrats, therefore, used their pivotal position to sustain Helmut Schmidt, who continued in power.

How different the outcome would have been if Germany used the British electoral system. Assuming that voting patterns did not change, the Christian Democrats would have had an assured overall majority in the Commons of at least 60 seats, and probably a good deal more. Helmut Kohl, the Christian Democrat leader, would have become Chancellor six years before he actually attained that position, and Helmut Schmidt would have been relegated to Opposition. The Free Democrats would have secured only a small handful of seats – when, in 1970, the British Liberals gained 7.5 per cent of the vote, they won only six seats in the Commons – and in any case they would have lost their pivotal position, since the Christian Democrats, with an overall majority in Parliament, would not need their support.

By 1980 the result in Germany was much closer. The Christian Democrat vote had fallen, but it was still the leading party.

CDU/CSU	44.5%
SPD	42.9%
FDP	10.6%

Again the Christian Democrats were frustrated in their

attempt to become the Government. The seats in the Bundestag were allocated as follows:

CDU/CSU	226 seats
SPD	218 seats
FDP	53 seats

The FDP once more used its pivotal position to support the SPD Chancellor, Helmut Schmidt, who continued to rule until October 1982, when the Free Democrats finally decided to change sides and support the Christian Democrats, so allowing Helmut Kohl finally to become Chancellor.

It is more difficult, in the case of the 1980 election, to conduct our thought experiment and imagine what the result would have been under the British electoral system, but there is a strong possibility that the CDU/CSU would just have secured an overall majority. Their lead of 1.6 per cent over the SPD would probably have given them at least 16 seats more than the Social Democrats: while the FDP with 10.6 per cent of the vote – a smaller percentage than the Liberals secured in 1979 (see p. 9) when they won 11 seats in the Commons – would probably not have won the party sufficient seats to hold the balance of power.

Now, in 1980 the Christian Democrat's candidate for Chancellor was not Helmut Kohl, but Franz-Josef Strauss, the leader of the Bavarian wing of the party, a man generally regarded as far to the right of Kohl and other Christian Democrat leaders. Many of those in Britain who followed German affairs were anxious lest the election of Strauss as Chancellor lead to instability in German politics, with an unsettling effect upon the Western Alliance. There was some relief, therefore, when he was defeated. When the election result was announced *The Times* published a leading article congratulating the German electorate on its maturity in rejecting Strauss and endorsing the more moderate and predictable Helmut Schmidt.

Yet, as we have seen, Strauss was rejected by the electoral system rather than the electorate. Under the British system he might well have been Chancellor. Conversely, James

Callaghan, who went down to ignominious defeat in 1979, might have been able to survive under a proportional system. Perhaps he would have been able to form a coalition with the Liberals, as Helmut Schmidt had done in Germany. The 'ifs' are endless.

We have now spent enough time on our various thought experiments to bring home the first point which this book is concerned to make. The electoral system which a country uses is vital in determining how the votes cast by electors are transformed into seats in the legislature. There is nothing automatic about the way in which votes are converted into seats, and different electoral systems will perform this function in different ways. This will affect the political colour of a country's Government, the relative strength of the various parties in the legislature, as well possibly as the identity of the Prime Minister.

Clearly, then, the electoral system which a country adopts will exert significant effects upon its political life. Let us therefore consider, in a little more detail, how the British electoral system actually works. Then we shall look at the main alternative systems, including the most important varieties of proportional representation. Only after that will we be in a position to consider the relative merits and defects of the different systems.

2

The British Electoral System

How the Electoral System Works

We have already noticed the first and, in some ways, the most important feature of the British electoral system – its tendency to exaggerate the support of the party with the most votes. As we have seen, the last two general elections in Britain, in 1979 and 1983, failed to produce Governments supported by a *majority of the votes cast*. Instead, they produced Governments supported by the *largest minority among the electorate*. In this the general elections of 1979 and 1983 were no different from every other general election since the war, none of which resulted in a Government supported by a majority of the voters. The electoral system, then, transforms a party with the *largest minority of the vote* into one with an *overall majority of the seats*. By augmenting the support of the largest party, it makes possible a majority Government in the Commons, even though that Government enjoys the support of less than half the electorate.

The British system generally ensures that the party with the most votes almost always gains the most seats. There have been only two occasions this century when this has not been the case. The first was in 1951, when Labour gained more votes than the Conservatives but the Conservatives won more seats, so ousting the post-war Labour Government from office. The second was in February 1974, when, by contrast, Labour was the beneficiary, for the Conservatives succeeded in gaining more votes than Labour, but Labour won more seats, ejecting Edward Heath's Government from office. At every other general election, however, the winning party in terms of seats has also been the winning party in terms of votes. If that were not the case, if the system produced quite random results bearing little relationship to the number of votes cast, then, obviously, it would have been discarded long ago.

The British electoral system works in a reasonably predictable manner. The principal reason for this is that supporters of the Conservative and Labour parties are not distributed randomly across the country but are residentially segregated; this means that Conservative voters are concentrated mainly in one set of constituencies, Labour voters in another set. The Conservatives are strongest in the rural areas and in the affluent suburbs, and in 1983 they won almost every seat in those parts of the country. Labour, by contrast, is strongest in the industrial conurbations. Even in so bad a year as 1983 Labour still succeeded in winning five out of the six seats in Liverpool and 10 out of the 11 seats in Glasgow, while the Conservatives, despite their landslide, could not win a single seat in either city. Hence even in a year when there is a massive victory for one party, the Opposition will still retain a considerable number of seats in its main areas of electoral strength.

Thus the British electoral system ensures both that the most popular party will win the most seats in the Commons and also that the winning party will usually gain enough seats to form a single-party majority Government. Since 1945 Britain has enjoyed single-party majority government for all but three and a half years, and only one general election – that of February 1974 – failed to produce a Government with an overall majority. The election of October 1974 yielded a Labour Government with a small overall majority of three, insufficient for the duration of the whole Parliament. By April 1976 this majority had been lost through a by-election defeat and a defection, and from then until the Government was finally defeated in the general election of May 1979 there was a minority Government. Apart from those two occasions, however, Britain has been governed by single-party majorities since the war.

A further consequence of the British electoral system is that it tends, in general, to penalize minor parties, that is, parties getting less than around 35 per cent of the vote. The clearest example of this has been the way in which the electoral system has treated the Liberals – and, in 1983, the Liberal/SDP Alliance – in the last four general elections. Table 3 compares the Liberals' share of the vote with their share of the seats.

TABLE 3   *Liberal votes and seats, 1974–83*

Election	% vote	No. of seats	% of seats
February 1974	19.3	14	2.2
October 1974	18.3	13	2.0
1979	13.8	11	1.7
1983 (Liberal/SDP Alliance)	25.4	23	3.5

The basic reason why the electoral system has treated the Liberal Party (and now treats the Alliance) so brutally is that electoral support for the Liberals and the Alliance is fairly evenly spread and is not concentrated in particular areas, as is the case with the Labour and Conservative parties. In the 1983 general election, for example, the Alliance vote in every region of the country was within 2 per cent of its average vote. Thus the Alliance was able to secure a large number of second places but unable to win more than a handful of constituencies. The Alliance would be more fortunately placed if, like the Labour and Conservative parties, it had peaks of strength in particular regions of the country, even though it did very badly in other areas. It was because the Labour vote was structured in this way that Labour secured over nine times as many seats as the Alliance on only a slightly higher vote. At the same time Labour was second in only 132 constituencies as compared with the Alliance's 314 second places, and it gained less than one-eighth of the vote, thereby losing its £150 deposit, in 119 seats as compared with the Alliance's 11 lost deposits.

The electoral system does not discriminate equally against all minor parties, however. The extent to which such parties are under-represented depends upon the way in which their vote is distributed. Parties whose support is highly concentrated in particular regions, such as the nationalist parties in Scotland and Wales, and the Northern Ireland parties, will not find themselves so seriously discriminated against. Indeed, if their vote is very highly concentrated, they may even enjoy slight over-representation.

In the general election of 1983 Plaid Cymru secured two seats – 0.3 per cent of the Commons total – for 0.4 per cent of the vote. This is because its vote is highly concentrated in the Welsh-speaking areas of north-west Wales. Thus Plaid Cymru gained less than one-eighth of the vote (losing its deposit) in no fewer than 32 out of the 38 Welsh seats, but still succeeded in winning two seats and coming close in two others.

The two general elections of 1974 provide further examples of how different types of third party are treated differently by the electoral system. In February 1974, as we have seen, the Liberals secured 14 seats on 19.3 per cent of the vote, but the Ulster Unionists, with 1.3 per cent of the total United Kingdom vote, were over-represented, gaining 11 seats (1.7 per cent) of the seats in the Commons. In October 1974 the Liberals, with 18.3 per cent of the vote, gained 13 seats, while the Scottish Nationalists, with 2.9 per cent of the total United Kingdom vote, secured 11 seats (1.7 per cent of the total).

The generalization that the British electoral system discriminates against third parties therefore needs to be qualified. It discriminates against a third party to the extent that a third party's vote is evenly distributed across the country. Thus even if the Alliance had gained more votes than Labour in 1983, it would still have won fewer seats. If the Alliance had won an extra 10 per cent of the vote, with this extra support coming evenly from Labour and the Conservatives, it would still have won only a further 29 seats, giving it 52 out of the 650 seats in the Commons (8 per cent of the seats) for 35 per cent (over one-third) of the vote.

Before the 1983 election various simulations were made to calculate how many seats each party would gain on various divisions of the vote. One such simulation* showed that if each political grouping gained 33 per cent of the vote, then the outcome in terms of seats would be:

Labour	290 seats
Conservatives	260 seats
Alliance	79 seats

Labour and the Conservatives would do so much better than the Alliance precisely because their votes were more concentrated in particular areas of the country, with Labour's vote being more concentrated than that of the Conservatives, who would be vulnerable to any advance of the Alliance.

Because, in general, it imposes a handicap on third parties, the British electoral system not only artificially manufactures an overall majority in the Commons for one party; it also tends towards the creation and maintenance of a *two-party system*. The electoral system helps the Conservative and Labour parties to maintain their dominance of seats in the Commons, even when, as in 1983, they are supported by only 70 per cent of the electorate.

It is not, of course, impossible for a third party to break through; otherwise the Labour Party would never have succeeded in becoming a major party in the state. Formed in 1900, its early years were spent in alliance with the Liberals, and it did not become a truly independent party until 1918. Yet the general election of that year made it the largest single Opposition party, and by 1924 it had formed its first Government, relegating the Liberals to the position of third party from which they have not yet been able to recover.

* David Butler, 'Variants of the Westminster Model', in Vernon Bogdanor and David Butler (eds.), *Democracy and Elections* (Cambridge, CUP, 1983), p. 47.

Perhaps the Liberal/SDP Alliance may be able to reverse the process which occurred between 1918 and 1924, turning the tables on Labour, so that the Alliance rather than Labour becomes the official Opposition to the Conservatives. At the time of writing, it is impossible to say whether or not this will happen. All that we can say with confidence is that the electoral system imposes a handicap upon the Alliance as it tries to become the second political grouping in the state – although, as the experience of the Labour Party in the 1920s shows, the handicap is not an insurmountable one.

We can now sum up our discussion of the main effects of the British electoral system by putting forward three propositions. The British electoral system will, first, reward the winning party in a general election by giving it an overall majority of seats for a minority of the popular vote; secondly, it will discriminate against minor parties whose support is not highly concentrated territorially; and finally, as a result, it will tend to the formation and maintenance of a two-party system.

A Three-Party System?

Not only does the British electoral system encourage the formation and maintenance of a two-party system, but it also works best when there are only two major parties competing for power. Between 1945 and 1974, when at every general election at least 87 per cent of those who voted supported Labour and the Conservatives, the system worked well in the sense that, except in 1951, the party with the most votes won the election and, in a very rough and ready way, the outcome did represent the views of the electorate. Moreover, until the 1970s the parties were much closer together in their views than they have since become. Consensus politics – agreement between the parties on fundamentals – was the norm, and the Labour and Conservative parties were led by their centrist wings, the right of the Labour Party, and the left of the Conservatives. Therefore it mattered less, perhaps, that one party had an artificial majority in the Commons, one which was not based upon a majority in the country.

Some argued that a two-party system in which the parties competed for the centre ground was itself a product of the electoral system. The British electoral system, so it was suggested, motivated parties to become broad-based coalitions so as to embrace the largest possible segment of public opinion. It discouraged extremists and encouraged moderation in government.

Whether this argument is correct or not, there can be little doubt that differences between the parties have become sharper over the last decade. Possibly for this reason, the two major parties attract less support than they did in the 1960s. In the two general elections of 1974 only 75 per cent of the voters supported Labour or the Conservatives as compared with over 87 per cent in the 1960s: by 1983 the figure was down to 70 per cent. When that happens the British electoral system is bound to work less well in representing electoral opinion. For the closer Britain gets to being a three-party system, the more tenuous the relationship between votes and seats.

We have seen that, with only the Labour and Conservative parties competing for power, the British system will yield a reasonably predictable and reliable relationship between votes and seats. This is because of what is, in a sense, a lucky accident: the fact that the supporters of the Labour and Conservative parties are distributed not randomly but in different clusters of constituencies. This gives each of the major parties their strongholds – their safe seats – and confines the electoral battle to the marginal seats whose socio-economic composition is generally mixed. It is because the two major parties are backed mainly by different social groups, and because these groups have different residence patterns, that the two-party system has given Britain electoral stability.

This stability is not inevitable. It results from what is a purely contingent factor, and it is undermined when a third political grouping such as the Alliance, whose support has an entirely different geographical distribution, cuts across the two-party system. It is for this reason that the election result in 1983 was the most anomalous that Britain has seen since the beginning of mass suffrage. Such results, moreover, are likely to continue for as long as three major groupings compete for power.

We have already seen (p. 18) that with an equal share-out of the vote between three groupings, Labour will have 30 more seats than the Conservatives and over 200 seats more than the Alliance. Labour gains more seats than the Conservatives because its vote is more highly concentrated in particular regions, because there are fewer marginal Labour seats, and because its seats are therefore less vulnerable to the threat of the Alliance. The Alliance does badly in terms of seats because of the very even distribution of its vote, which means that, below about 38 per cent of the vote it will always be severely under-represented in the House of Commons.

Above that level, however, the Alliance would gain seats in leaps and bounds. If the Alliance were to gain 45 per cent of the vote, it could be the beneficiary of a massive landslide. If the vote were distributed as follows:

Alliance	45%
Conservative	27%
Labour	25%
Others (Nationalists and Northern Ireland parties)	3%

and if there were an even swing in different parts of the country to the Alliance, then the seats would be distributed as follows: *

Alliance	467 seats
Conservative	24 seats
Labour	135 seats
Others	24 seats

* This simulation, together with those following, was prepared by Clive Payne of the Computing Unit of the Social Studies Faculty at Oxford University.

The Conservatives, as shown above, would have over 100 fewer seats than Labour, despite having gained 2 per cent more of the vote. This, of course, would be a consequence of the fact that Conservative seats would be more vulnerable than Labour seats to the Alliance; much of the Labour vote would still be concentrated in safe seats, allowing the Labour vote to fall without so many seats being lost.

The Alliance vote, therefore, is relatively *elastic* with respect to increases in its vote *over 38 per cent*, since the number of seats which it receives increases very rapidly indeed with every extra 1 per cent of the vote beyond that level, but its vote is relatively *inelastic* with respect to increases in its vote *up to the level of around 35 per cent*, since it is not until the Alliance reaches this level that it can begin to make a breakthrough in terms of seats. The Conservative vote is less elastic than that of the Alliance but more elastic than Labour's. But if the Conservative vote were to fall below around 30 per cent, the party would start to lose seats very rapidly indeed.

The Labour Party's vote is, however, rather more fortunately distributed from the point of view of a three-party contest, for, at about 25–41 per cent of the vote, it is relatively *inelastic* with respect both to increases and to decreases. This means that, as we have seen, the Labour vote can fall below 30 per cent – as it did in the 1983 general election – without the party suffering too severe a loss of seats.

Because of this inelasticity Labour could easily become the largest party in the Commons on a very small percentage of the vote. Consider the following distribution of votes and seats:

	% Vote	Seats
Labour	30	256
Conservative	30	184
Alliance	37	185
Others	3	25

while with only 37 per cent of the vote, Labour could quite easily come very near to securing an overall majority of the seats.

	% Vote	Seats
Labour	37	323
Conservative	30	238
Alliance	30	64
Others	3	25

The disadvantage which Labour suffers from the structure of its vote is that it needs a much higher percentage of the vote than the Conservatives or the Alliance would need to gain a landslide. But in recent years, Labour has not looked remotely like achieving a landslide, and what has been important to the party has been the way in which the electoral system has cushioned its loss of support and has helped it to remain one of the two major parties in the British political system. Indeed, in none of the last four general elections – February 1974, October 1974, 1979 and 1983 – has the Labour Party been able to secure as much as 40 per cent of the vote, yet on two of these occasions, February and October 1974, it was able to form the Government, while in 1979 and 1983 it was the major Opposition party to the Conservatives in the Commons.

It will be seen from the simulations discussed above that in a system in which three political groupings compete for power the results of a general election can diverge a long way from an accurate reflection of the opinions of voters. It is worth emphasizing that these outcomes depend not upon any extravagant or pathological assumptions, but only upon the simplifying assumption of an even national swing and the absence of regional swings such as might distort the overall result.

It is clear, then, that the nearer the three parties come to sharing the vote between them, the more volatile and unpredictable the relationship between seats and votes will be. At present it is the Alliance which finds itself the victim of the electoral system, and it is in the interests of the Alliance, rather than of Labour or the Conservatives, to press for change. However, the Conservative and Labour parties are in a more dangerous position than they might at present think, for, as the example on p. 21 shows, the Conservatives are highly vulnerable to an advance of the Alliance, which could make them the third party in terms of seats in the House of Commons. Indeed, this is what would happen if in a general election the Conservatives were to perform as badly as they did in 1981, when their support, according to opinion polls, fell to only 27 per cent. Further, Conservative supporters face the problem that if the Conservative vote falls, a relatively small upsurge in the Labour vote could make Labour the largest party in the Commons. If the precedent of 1974 is anything to go by, Labour in that situation would form a minority Government, implementing policies to which Conservatives are strongly opposed. During the period 1974–9, many Conservatives objected to such policies as the abolition of paybeds in National Health hospitals, the extension of comprehensive education and legislation increasing the influence of the trade unions. Conservatives argued that such measures could not be justified by a Government which had the support of under 40 per cent of the voters, and Lord Hailsham, the Conservative Party's elder statesman, argued that British government was approaching the condition of an 'elective dictatorship'. Yet Conservatives can have no guarantee that such a situation will not recur.

Labour, on the other hand, now finds that its bitter opponent, Mrs Thatcher, enjoys a vast overall majority on just over two-fifths of the vote. Obviously, Labour supporters hope that their party will be able to recover, but unless it can do so rapidly, anti-Conservative voters may have to grow used to Conservative Governments implementing policies which they utterly reject on a minority of the popular vote. Both Labour and the Alliance need a huge increase on their 1983 level of support to form a majority Government, while the split in the anti-Conservative vote could allow the Conservatives to continue governing, on a minority vote, for many years to come. That cannot be in the interests of the Labour Party. Labour may have to face the question of whether its dislike of Mrs Thatcher outweighs its dislike of proportional representation. If party self-interest is a guide, therefore, it is perfectly possible for both Conservative and Labour supporters to reach the conclusion that retention of the existing electoral system is no longer in their interests.

The advent of a strong third political grouping in Britain thus illuminates one of the basic weaknesses in the British electoral system. It emphasizes the fact that, under this system, the number of seats which a party wins depends not only upon how many votes it receives but also upon the geographical distribution of these votes, upon where the votes are cast. Because of this the continued existence of three political groupings in Britain is likely to lead to further election results like those of 1983, in which the allocation of seats in the Commons is very far from being an accurate reflection of the level of support for each of the three parties in the country.

For this very reason, there are many who would argue that, in a country using the first-past-the-post electoral system, three major political groupings cannot survive to compete against each other for very long. The three-party system, some would suggest, represents merely a transitional stage in the evolution of the British party system. Either the Alliance will come to replace Labour as the main Opposition or, alternatively, Labour will recover its strength and the Alliance will become a small minor grouping, as the Liberals were in the 1950s and 1960s. Certainly, Britain has never for long had a system in which three equal parties were competing for the vote. What seemed a three-party system in the 1920s proved to mark a period of transition between the decline of the Liberals and the rise of Labour. Nor has any other country which uses the British electoral system ever sustained a structure comprising three nearly equal parties for long, for if a three-party system turns out to be not transitional but permanent, then the electoral system comes to be altered so that it can accommodate three parties. This is what happened, for example, in

Belgium, the first country to adopt proportional representation as a method of electing its legislature in 1899. Until the 1890s party competition in Belgium was restricted to a Liberal and a Catholic party, but in 1894 a socialist party threatened the position of the two older parties. Election results could have become quite unpredictable, and it was in the interests of all three parties to change the electoral system to one of proportional representation. It is clear, therefore, that if Britain retains a party system in which three political groupings compete for power, then the pressure to change the electoral system will become very strong, for however well the system works with two parties, for which it was designed, it operates far less satisfactorily when there are three.

A Divided Nation?

So far we have noted that the British electoral system exaggerates the support of the winning party in an election, under-represents minor parties whose support is not territorially concentrated and contains within itself pressures tending towards a two-party system. It is now worth looking at how the electoral system works in reflecting opinion in different regions of the country.

Just as the British electoral system tends to exaggerate the support of the winning party in the country as a whole, so also it exaggerates the support of the winning party in a particular region. We can see this by taking a map of England and drawing a line to connect the Wash and the River Severn. If we consider the area south of that line, excluding Greater London, we find that there are 179 parliamentary constituencies within the area. In the general election of 1983, however, out of those 179 only three Labour MPs were returned – those from Ipswich, Thurrock and Bristol South. If we were to draw a second line to connect Bristol with Dover, we would find that there were no Labour MPs at all south of the line.

This does not, of course, mean that no one votes Labour south of the line from the Wash to the Severn. In fact, around 17 per cent – one-sixth of those who voted – supported Labour within this area. But these voters were unsuccessful in securing representation. Similarly, in the general election of 1979, in the south-east region of England, excluding Greater London, Labour secured only four seats, although it gained around one-quarter of the vote within the region. In 1983, there was a similar imbalance in representation:

	% Votes	Seats
Conservatives	54.2	106
Alliance	29.1	1
Labour	16.0	1

Conversely, in areas where Labour is strong the Conservatives will find themselves under-represented. Despite their landslide victory in 1983, the Conservatives were still unable to win any seats in two of Britain's largest conurbations, Liverpool and Glasgow. Again, this does not mean that no one voted Conservative in Liverpool or Glasgow. In Liverpool, for example, nearly 30 per cent of those voting supported the Conservatives, but they were not able to secure representation – although, paradoxically, the Alliance, which was the third party in Liverpool with only 19 per cent of the vote, *did* succeed in winning a seat. So, just as Labour is under- represented in the south of England, the Conservatives find themselves under-represented in the major industrial cities of the north. If we consider the eight major industrial cities north of Birmingham – Bradford, Glasgow, Hull, Leeds, Liverpool, Manchester, Newcastle, and Sheffield – we find that of the 43 constituencies within these cities, the Conservatives hold just six.

The British electoral system, therefore, under-represents not only minor parties but also major parties which come second in particular regions of the country. There is, of course, a disparity between the support for Labour and the Conservatives in different regions of the country. The Conservatives are stronger in the south of England than they are in Glasgow and Liverpool, and Labour is stronger in Glasgow and Liverpool than it is in the south, but the electoral system aggravates this disparity, making it appear as if every voter in the south of England supports the Conservatives, while every voter in Glasgow and Liverpool supports Labour.

This has important consequences for the development of party policies. The Conservatives, lacking representation in the large industrial conurbations of the north come to be insufficiently aware of the problems of the inner cities to be able to deal with them effectively. The inner-city riots of 1981 took many Conservative Ministers by surprise. The Government's response was to give Michael Heseltine, then Secretary of State for the Environment, responsibility for Merseyside. Heseltine made a series of well publicized visits to Liverpool, and at the 1981 Conservative Conference he appealed to the delegates to recognize the difficulties faced by those who lived in Britain's inner cities. But it might have been easier for the Conservative Government to understand these problems if there had been Conservative MPs from the inner cities able to acquaint Ministers with the situation. 'The central obstacle to solving the inner-city problem under a Conservative Government,' according to Paul Harrison, author of a recent book on the problems of Hackney, 'is, I believe, lack of awareness. Tory MPs and Ministers, representing more prosperous suburban and county areas, can have little conception of the intolerable human realities of life in the inner cities.'*

Conversely, the Labour Party, lacking representation in the more prosperous parts of the country, may be less sensitive to developments there. For example, Labour MPs may be insufficiently aware of the issues raised by the new micro-technological industries whose base is in the south of England. Labour is often accused of concentrating its attention too much on the problems of the declining industries of the north of England and not producing policies relevant to the indus-

* 'The moral bombshell in our city centres', *Sunday Times*, 21 August 1983.

tries of the future. That could be a consequence of Labour's geographical base, which is so heavily skewed towards the north that it has hardly any MPs living in the areas where the new technology is taking root.

It is clear then, that there are many defects in the British electoral system. That in itself is not surprising. No political institution is perfect, and electoral systems are no exception to that rule. If the search for an alternative to the British electoral system is a search for the perfect system, it will be doomed from the start, for there is no such system. Every electoral system known to man has its share of defects and anomalies. The question therefore, is not which electoral system is the perfect one but rather which electoral system, in the light of Britain's current political situation, has the smallest number of defects, and is the least likely to produce anomalies. Before we can hope to answer this question, we must examine the main alternative electoral systems, weighing their merits and defects against those of the British. Only then can we hope to reach a balanced verdict.

3

The Alternative Vote and the Two-Ballot System

The Alternative Vote

There are a very large number of alternative electoral systems. As long ago as 1910 a Royal Commission appointed to inquire into electoral systems – the only Royal Commission ever to have been set up in Britain with such a remit – claimed that there were over 300 different systems, either actual or potential. Human ingenuity being what it is, there are probably many more than 300 systems today.

Fortunately, there is not the slightest need to discuss even a fraction of those systems. Many of them are, in fact, variations on simple basic types, combining and recombining the same elements together in different ways. Others, for various reasons, are generally agreed, even by advocates of electoral change, to be quite unsuited to British conditions, and we need not spend time analysing them.

We shall confine ourselves to discussing just four different systems. In the next two chapters we shall consider the two main varieties of proportional representation which have been recommended for use in Britain. These are the proportional system used in the Federal Republic of Germany, which we shall call the 'German system': it is sometimes also called the additional member system for reasons which will become apparent. Second, there is the system of proportional representation used in the Irish Republic and also for local government elections in Northern Ireland and known as the 'single transferable vote'. If Britain were ever to adopt proportional representation, it would probably be one of these two systems that she would select.

In this chapter, however, we shall consider two electoral systems, which, although not examples of proportional representation, have been recommended by some electoral reformers as methods of avoiding one of the anomalies of the British electoral system. These two systems are the *alternative vote*, which is used to elect the Australian lower house, roughly corresponding to our House of Commons, and the *two-ballot system*, used to elect both the French President and the French lower house. It is with this latter example of its use that we shall be concerned.

The anomaly which both of these systems seek to avoid is that by which, under the British electoral system, a candidate can win a constituency even though he does not receive the support of the majority of the voters in the constituency. If there are only two candidates in a constituency, then, of course, a candidate must secure over 50 per cent of the vote to win, but in the 1983 general election there was no constituency in which only two candidates competed for election. In 253 constituencies there were three candidates; in 250 constituencies there were four candidates; while in the remaining 147 constituencies there were more than four candidates. This means that MPs can be returned to Parliament on less than 50 per cent of the vote. In 1983, 336 seats – over half of the total of 650 – were won by candidates securing under 50 per cent of the vote, while 70 candidates were returned on less than 40 per cent of the vote. In extreme circumstances one can obtain a result such as the following, which occurred in the October 1974 general election in the constituency of East Dunbartonshire:

	No. of votes	% vote
Mrs M. Bain (Scottish National Party)	15,551	31.2
J. S. B. Henderson (Conservative)	15,529	31.1
E. F. McGarry (Labour)	15,122	30.3
J. A. Thompson (Liberal)	3,626	7.3

Mrs Bain was returned as an MP even though she had the support of only 31.2 per cent of her constituents. If Labour, Liberal or Conservative voters had been aware that this might happen, they might well have cast their votes for the candidate whom they thought could most easily defeat Mrs Bain. As the SNP candidate, Mrs Bain was, after all, in favour of an independent Scotland, and the vast majority of those who voted Labour, Liberal or Conservative must have been opposed to this notion. Liberal voters, for example, might well have preferred a Conservative Member of Parliament, who would at least be committed to the preservation of the United Kingdom, to an MP pledged to work for its dissolution. In the British electoral system, however, it is impossible to exercise a second choice; nor, of course, can the anti-SNP voter know in advance where his vote can be used most effectively to bring about the defeat of the SNP candidate.

Such constituency victories on a minority vote have been increasing in recent years, as minor parties have gained in strength. In 1951 and 1955 only 39 and 37 seats respectively were won on a minority vote, but since 1959 the number has only twice been below 200. The largest number of seats won on a minority vote was in February 1974, when no fewer than 408 seats – nearly two-thirds of the 635 seats in the Commons – were won on minority votes, while in the general election of 1983, as we have seen, the figure was 336. (The total number of seats in the Commons was raised from 635 to 650 for the general election of 1983.)

Both the alternative vote and two-ballot electoral system attempt to avoid the possibility that any MP will be elected on a minority vote. They seek to achieve this aim through different means: the alternative vote by allowing the expression of preferences for second and, if necessary, further choices in addition to the voter's first choice of candidate; the two-ballot system by providing for a second ballot to be held if no candidate has secured an absolute majority of the vote on the first.

Form F

(To be initialled on back by Presiding Officer before issue)

BALLOT PAPER

COMMONWEALTH OF AUSTRALIA
STATE OF TASMANIA

Electoral Division of DENISON

Election of One Member of the House of Representatives

DIRECTIONS.—Mark your vote on this ballot-paper by placing the numbers **1, 2, 3** and **4** in the squares respectively opposite the names of the candidates so as to indicate the order of your preference for them.

CANDIDATES

☐   **COATES, John**

☐   **HAY, John Charles**

☐   **HODGMAN, Michael**

☐   **STANTON, Cathryn Marie**

FIGURE 1   *A specimen Australian ballot paper*

The alternative vote, as used in Australia, requires the voter to mark his ballot paper not with an 'X' as in Britain but with a '1' by his most favoured candidate, a '2' by the one he next favours and so on until he has put a number against every candidate on the ballot paper (see figure 1). Voting is compulsory in Australia, and if the alternative vote were ever to be adopted in Britain, it would probably be modified so that no voter would be required to do more than mark a '1' by his most favoured candidate for his vote to be valid. He would not have to express a preference for every candidate.

When voting has been completed, first-preference votes are counted. If any candidate has an absolute majority (over 50 per cent) of the vote, he is elected. If, however, no candidate has succeeded in reaching 50 per cent of the vote, then the candidate at the bottom of the poll is eliminated, and his second-preference votes are added on to the first-preference votes of the remaining candidates. It may then be the case that one candidate has more than 50 per cent of the total vote and, if so, he is declared elected. If, however, there is still no candidate with an absolute majority of the vote, then the candidate now at the bottom of the poll is eliminated and his second-preference votes redistributed. This process continues until a candidate finally succeeds in obtaining an absolute majority.

Let us conduct an imaginary experiment on the October 1974 East Dunbartonshire result (p. 31), making some assumptions about the distribution of second and third preferences. Let us assume that the actual result represents only first-preference votes. It is clear that no candidate is within reach of 50 per cent of the vote. Therefore we eliminate the candidate at the bottom of the poll, the Liberal, Thompson. Let us assume that his second preferences are marked as follows:

10% (i.e. 362 votes) for the SNP candidate
25% (i.e. 906 votes) for the Conservative candidate
25% (i.e. 906 votes) for the Labour candidate

The remaining 40 per cent (i.e. 1,452) of Thompson's votes are, let us assume, not marked with any further preferences.

The situation will then be as follows:

Mrs Bain (Scottish National Party) $15,551 + 362 = 15,913$
J. S. B. Henderson (Conservative) $15,529 + 906 = 16,435$
E. F. McGarry (Labour) $15,122 + 906 = 16,028$

It is clear that no candidate has yet secured 50 per cent of the vote, and we must therefore eliminate the candidate with the least number of votes. This is now Mrs Bain. Let us assume that her votes are distributed as follows:

 5% for the Conservative candidate
25% for the Labour candidate
30% for the Liberal candidate
40% expressing no further preference

Since the Liberal candidate is already eliminated, however, there is no point in allocating any further votes to him. So, looking at the *third* preferences of the 30 per cent of Mrs Bain's first preferences whose second preference was for the Liberal, let us assume that we find:

10% for the Conservative candidate
10% for the Labour candidate
10% expressing no further preference

The totals for the two remaining candidates are therefore:

$5\% + 10\% = 15\% = 15,913 \times 15\% = 2,387$ votes for the Conservative candidate
$25\% + 10\% = 35\% = 15,913 \times 35\% = 5,570$ votes for the Labour candidate

The remaining 50% of Mrs Bain's votes, (i.e. $15,913 \times 50\% = 7,956$ votes) express no further preference.

The situation will then be as follows:

J. S. B. Henderson (Conservative) $16,435 + 2,387 = 18,822$
E. F. McGarry (Labour) $16,028 + 5,570 = 21,598$

There being only two candidates left, McGarry, who now has the most votes, is declared elected. Thus the seat, on our hypothetical but not perhaps unreasonable assumptions, would have been won by the Labour candidate and not by the Scottish Nationalist.

If we look at the operation of the alternative vote over the country as a whole, however, rather than concentrating on a particular constituency, the result might be very different. In fact, it would probably be the Alliance which would benefit most from this system. This is because the Alliance, rather than Labour (or the Conservatives), would probably be the second choice of most voters. In constituencies where the Conservatives were third, Conservative voters would probably give their second vote to the Alliance rather than to Labour, while in constituencies where Labour was third, Labour voters would prefer the Alliance to the Conservatives. In the 1983 general election the Alliance was second in 314 seats, 265 of which were won by the Conservatives. Therefore the alternative vote would be likely to benefit the Alliance at the expense of the Conservatives. This could prove a mixed blessing for the Alliance, however, for some of its Members would be elected with the help of second-preference Conservative votes, while others would be elected with the help of second-preference Labour votes. This might make it more difficult for the Alliance to work out coherent policies of its own. The two parties comprising the Alliance might find themselves being tugged in two different directions, one by MPs dependent upon Conservative support, and the other by those dependent upon Labour support. As a grouping of the centre, the Alliance could easily find its political identity submerged by conflicting constituency pressures.

But the alternative vote system would in any case not be a very good one for Britain to adopt because it does not operate with any consistent degree of fairness. Since, however, the alternative vote shares this defect with the two-ballot system, we shall first describe the two-ballot system before showing that neither can really be defended as an improvement upon the British electoral system.

The Two-Ballot System

The two-ballot system, as used in elections to the French National Assembly, requires a second ballot to be held one week after the first if no candidate has succeeded in gaining 50 per cent of the vote on the first ballot. To enter the second ballot, however, a candidate must have secured votes of 12½ per cent of the *registered electorate* in the first ballot. Since in British general elections the voter turnout rate is generally between 80 and 70 per cent this is equivalent to securing between around 15½ and 17¾ per cent of the votes. With a turnout rate of 75 per cent, around 16⅔ per cent of the votes cast would be needed. In practice, however, there are usually only two candidates on the second ballot, since the political battle in France is fairly sharply polarized between two parties of the left – socialists and Communists – and two groupings of the right – Gaullists and a federation of non-Gaullist right-wing parties. The two blocks usually each agree on just one candidate from their respective camps to represent them on the second ballot, so as to avoid splitting the vote, for in the second ballot the candidate with the most votes is elected, whether he has an absolute majority or not.

In the British context the two-ballot system might not work quite as straightforwardly as it does in France, where there is a clear polarization between left and right. For in most of Britain the political battle is not one of left versus right, but one of left, right and centre (counting the Alliance as a centre grouping), complicated in Scotland and in parts of Wales by the presence of strong nationalist candidates. Thus, under the rules which obtain in France, in our example of East Dunbartonshire (p. 31) only the Liberal candidate would be ineligible to stand in the second ballot. It is highly unlikely that any of the remaining three candidates could agree among themselves on who should stand down. Therefore, the possibility is that all three would stand in the second ballot, and the winning candidate would still be elected by under 50 per cent of the vote.

Further, if we assume that the preferences of those who voted Liberal are the same as they were in our hypothetical example of the alternative vote (p. 34), then on the second ballot it would be the Conservative and not the Labour candidate who would win the election, for the result of the second ballot would be as at the top of p. 35. So, in the absence of party agreement, a less representative candidate could be returned under the two-ballot system than under the alternative vote.

However, the two-ballot system would have the advantage over the alternative vote in that voters would be able to *see* what the tactical situation was after the first ballot; they would not have to *guess* what it might be, as under the alternative vote. In the East Dunbartonshire example, for instance, before casting their vote in a second ballot voters would be able to see that the Liberal had been eliminated and that the SNP candidate was very marginally in the lead. On the evidence of the first ballot, the Conservative would be seen to have the better chance of stopping the SNP candidate, since he had 400 more votes than Labour. Thus a fervent upholder of the Union between Scotland and England in East Dunbartonshire would know that if he wished, at all costs, to prevent the SNP candidate from winning, it would be better to vote Conservative than to vote Labour. This would make it easier for the voter to cast his vote so as to exert maximum influence upon the outcome.

As compared with the alternative vote, however, the second ballot is more likely to encourage unnatural party bargaining. To revert again to our East Dunbartonshire example, once the first ballot result was known, supporters of the SNP, Conservatives and Labour would seek to bargain with the Liberal candidate in order to secure Liberal votes on the second ballot. Perhaps Labour, for example, might try to arrange a bargain with the SNP whereby, if Labour stood down in East Dunbartonshire and called upon its supporters to vote SNP, the SNP would correspondingly stand down in another constituency where Labour was in the lead.

MPs elected by such unholy alliances might, as with the alternative vote, be seriously handicapped in their parliamentary careers by the need to compromise with other, opposed, parties upon whose support they depended. Some Labour MPs, for example, might depend on SNP votes, others on Liberal votes. That might not make for very cohesive political parties or for very successful government.

Avoiding the Split Vote

Despite the difference in voting methods, the alternative vote and the two-ballot system share the common aim of ensuring that no candidate can win a seat on a minority of the vote. Further, they prevent the artificial limitation of candidatures which arises under the British electoral system through fear of splitting the vote. When, for example, the Liberals and SDP sought an electoral alliance, they had to engage in cumbrous and difficult negotiations to divide the constituencies between them, so that in half the constituencies there was a Liberal candidate and in the other half a candidate representing the SDP. It was not possible for Liberals and SDP candidates to run together in a constituency, since they would be fighting each other, thus splitting the vote and making it easier for their Labour or Conservative opponent to take the seat.

One consequence of this is that many voters will not support the candidate of their first choice if they feel that he or she is unlikely to win, so as not to hand the seat to the candidate of the major party whom they most dislike. To take an example: in a constituency which is marginal as between the Conservative and Labour parties, a Liberal voter who is strongly anti-socialist faces a dilemma. If he votes for his preferred choice of a Liberal candidate, he is in danger of letting in the Labour candidate and wasting his vote. Therefore he may vote tactically for the Conservative so as to keep Labour out. If he does this, however, he reduces the support of the candidate he really prefers – the Liberal – and the total votes for the various candidates will no longer be a reflection of their real support among voters.

Under either the alternative vote or the two-ballot system, however, any number of candidates can stand without any danger of splitting the vote. Liberal and SDP candidates could stand together in every constituency, allowing the voter to choose which he preferred. Under the alternative vote, the voter could list his preferences without any fear that he will be handing the seat to a party which he bitterly opposes. Under the two-ballot system, the two parties – Liberal and SDP – could agree that whichever party was behind after the first ballot should stand down in favour of the other on the second. It would even be possible (although it hardly ever happens where these two systems are in operation) for two candidates from the same party to stand if they represent different viewpoints. It would, for example, be possible for a left-wing and a right-wing Labour candidate both to stand, allowing the voter to choose between them. Thus under both the alternative vote and the two-ballot system greater choice would be available to the elector than is possible under the British system, and the need for tactical voting – voting for a candidate who is not one's first choice in order to keep out a candidate to whom one is bitterly opposed – would become less prevalent.

The Alternative Vote and the Two-Ballot System as Systems of Disproportional Representation

The alternative vote and, less frequently, the two-ballot system are often recommended by those who find defects in the British electoral system but do not wish to go as far as to support one of the proportional systems. For, as we shall see, almost all systems of proportional representation require *either* multi-member constituencies *or* party lists of candidates who do not stand for election in any constituency at all but become MPs solely because they enjoy the support of their party organization.

Further, unlike any scheme of proportional representation, the alternative vote and two-ballot systems would be much less likely to lead to either a coalition or a minority Government. The only general elections since the war when the alternative vote might have changed a decisive result into an indecisive one were 1964 and October 1974. On each occasion Labour, instead of winning a small absolute majority, would almost certainly have remained the largest party but without an absolute majority.

Despite these advantages, however, there is one striking weakness which the alternative vote and two-ballot systems share. They do not ensure that the results of general elections reflect the number of votes cast for each party. This can be seen from the following examples of elections in Australia and France.

In Australia the alternative vote allows two anti-socialist parties, the Liberal Party and the National Country Party, to fight as an electoral coalition against Labour, with each party putting up candidates in the same constituency and no danger of splitting the vote. The result of the 1977 general election for the House of Representatives in Australia was as follows:

	% votes	% seats
Labour	40.0	28.2
Liberals	38.3	53.2
National Country Party	9.7	14.5
Liberal/National Country Party coalition	= 48.0	= 67.7
Democrats	9.3	–
Others	2.7	–

It will be seen that the Liberals gained over 50 per cent of the seats, and therefore an absolute majority in the House of Representatives, with fewer votes than Labour, which secured just a little over a quarter of the seats. The Liberal/National Country Party coalition secured a large majority of the seats (over two-thirds) – a landslide victory – with only a minority of the popular vote.

In France, in the National Assembly elections of 1981, the parties of the non-Communist left — primarily the socialists — secured an absolute majority of the seats for only 38 per cent of the popular vote on the first ballot:

	% votes	% seats
Communists	16	9
Non-Communist left	38	62
Gaullists	21	15
Non-Gaullist right	22	14

In Britain, as we have seen, both the alternative vote and the two-ballot system would probably help the Alliance, the most likely second choice of both Labour and Conservative voters. The Alliance would, almost certainly, gain more seats from the Conservatives than from Labour. But the Conservative Party would be the more vulnerable to the Alliance, not because it benefits more from Britain's present electoral system than Labour but because of the accident of the geographical distribution of Conservative and Labour seats.

For this reason, the alternative vote or the two-ballot system would have led to election results reflecting opinion more accurately in elections such as those of 1970, 1979 or 1983, which the Conservatives won. In these elections the Conservatives benefited from the tendency of the British electoral system to give exaggerated majorities to the leading party. The alternative vote or the two-ballot system would assist the Alliance but mainly in seats where it could not harm Labour; and it would optimize the anti-Conservative vote.

On the other hand, in years such as 1966, when Labour gained an exaggerated majority, itself benefiting from this characteristic of the British electoral system, the alternative vote or two-ballot system would be likely to yield a *less* proportional result than Britain's present electoral system. The alternative vote or two-ballot system would actually increase Labour's overall majority in a year such as 1966.

Thus these systems would turn out to be biased against the Conservative Party, and they would make it easier for Labour to win an overall majority on a minority of the popular vote.

In Australia the distribution of safe and marginal seats is such that it is Labour which finds itself most threatened by the second preferences allowed under the alternative vote system. The alternative vote biases the result against the Australian Labour Party. Since 1949 the Australian Labour Party has received fewer seats than it would have done under the British electoral system at every general election except four; and in 1954 and 1961 the alternative vote kept Labour out of office, although Labour secured a higher percentage of the vote than the Liberal/National Country Party coalition.

Neither the alternative vote nor the two-ballot system, therefore, necessarily helps to secure a more accurate degree of representation than is offered by the British system. They do not ensure that the outcome, in terms of seats at a general election, accurately reflects the number of votes cast for each party; and indeed the advocates of these systems generally do not attempt to defend them on these grounds. The reason why these systems do not secure proportional representation is because the anomalies in the British electoral system which we noted in chapter 2 are not only – or not primarily – due to the existence of MPs elected on a minority vote. In Britain the Conservatives have won more seats on a minority vote at every general election since 1918, but they have been over-represented only in such general elections as 1979 and 1983, when they won overall majorities. In elections such as 1945 and 1966, however, when Labour won overall majorities, the Conservatives were under-represented even though they won more seats on a minority vote than Labour. So eliminating MPs elected on a minority vote would have further under-represented the Conservatives. The Conservatives win more seats than Labour on a minority vote not because the electoral system is necessarily biased towards them but because of the geographical distribution of their support.

Both the alternative vote and the two-ballot system share with the British electoral system the weakness that the number of seats which a party wins in a general election depends not only upon *how many* votes the party receives but also upon *where* these votes are cast. It is perfectly possible for every constituency to be won on a majority vote and yet for the outcome to fail to reflect the majority view of the voters. This will occur if one party piles up large majorities in safe seats, while a second party wins an equal number of seats by very small majorities. The first party will suffer from a large number of wasted votes – votes which do not contribute to the election of an MP.

It is sometimes suggested that such a distortion is solely a result of the inept (or deliberately biased) drawing of boundaries between constituencies. If only boundaries were drawn in a completely impartial way, it is argued, then the alternative vote or the two-ballot system would yield an accurate reflection of the wishes of electors.

But there may be no method of drawing boundaries which can prevent one party from piling up majorities in safe seats while another wins more seats, but on smaller majorities. There may, for example, be no way in which the boundaries of Glasgow can be redrawn so as to ensure that the Conservatives can win one of the 11 seats in the city for their one-sixth of the vote. In the general election in South Africa in 1948, for example, no seat was won on a minority vote, yet the United Party and its Labour Party allies gained 52 per cent of the vote and 71 seats, while their opponents, the Nationalist Party, with its allies, secured 42 per cent of the vote but gained 79 seats. Although there was some weighting in the size of the constituencies, with the Nationalists gaining an advantage from winning in constituencies with smaller electorates, this difference was far too small to explain such a glaring anomaly. The real reason for the result was that the United Party piled up huge majorities in urban seats, while the Nationalists won rural marginals. There were no fewer than 17 United or Labour Party majorities above the largest Nationalist majority of 4,025, and the Nationalists had 28 majorities below 1,000, while the United Party had only 12.*

The anomalies of the British electoral system, therefore, arise not because seats are won on a minority vote but because there is no reason why a constituency system – a *territorially based* system – should generate an outcome which is proportional between the parties. The British electoral system is based on geography and not upon proportionality. To secure proportionality, it is necessary to take the geography out of elections. This is something which neither the alternative vote nor the two-ballot system can do.

* Enid Lakeman, *How Democracies Vote*, 4th edn (London, Faber & Faber, 1974), p. 77.

4

Proportional Representation: The German System

Although proportional representation has been a major topic of political debate in Britain for the last decade, there are probably more misconceptions about it than about any other political issue. The most important of these misconceptions, which must be dispelled at the outset, is the one which treats 'proportional representation' as the name of a single electoral system. It is not. 'Proportional representation' refers not to a specific electoral system but to an *ideal* or *principle* to which different electoral systems seek to conform. There are, in fact, a very large number of proportional systems. Therefore whenever we talk about proportional representation, we should always specify which particular system we have in mind; the different systems work in different ways to achieve the common goal of proportionality, and they can have very different political consequences.

The second misconception about proportional representation is, perhaps, peculiar to Britain. It lies in thinking of the British electoral system as the norm and 'proportional representation' as something rather eccentric and odd. But proportional representation systems are far from being unusual. They are used by every European democracy except for Britain and France, and the majority of the world's stable democracies use one or other of the various systems of proportional representation.

Far from being the norm, the British system is often regarded by those on the Continent as a strange anomaly. Indeed, no major democracy which has not been under British rule actually uses the British system today. The question of whether or not Britain ought to retain her electoral system cannot, therefore, be decided simply by condemning proportional representation as the quirk of a deranged minority. We cannot assess proportional representation without first trying to understand it.

Although there are a very large number of proportional systems, only two have been seriously recommended for elections to the House of Commons: the German electoral system (together with a variant of it, which we shall also discuss), and the electoral system used in the Irish Republic and also in elections, other than those for the House of Commons, in Northern Ireland and known as the single tranferable vote.

The reason why serious discussion about proportional representation in Britain has been confined to these particular systems is that those who favour change are anxious that any system used for Westminster elections should preserve some of the familiar features of the British electoral system. In particular, reformers are anxious that a proportional system should preserve the virtues of the British constituency structure, with what is seen as a close relationship between the constituency and its representative, the MP. Any new system must be easy for the voter to understand and easy also to introduce. But, above all, any proportional system must provide for stable government. This means that it must not encourage the growth of numerous small parties unable to participate in government themselves but capable of rendering effective government impossible.

A system suitable for Britain, then, in the view of most electoral reformers, must attempt to strike a balance between the two aims of accurately reflecting votes cast and providing for stable and effective government. Most systems of proportional representation achieve the first aim, but some – the

Italian electoral system, or the Israeli, for example – do not secure the second very well. The German electoral system and the Irish (the single transferable vote) are, in the view of almost all supporters of proportional representation, the systems most suitable for adoption in Britain. They are, however, two quite different systems operating through dissimilar mechanisms. All that they have in common is the intention of relating seats to votes much more closely than the British electoral system permits.

In this chapter we will describe the German electoral system, and a variant of it which has also been recommended as suitable for Britain. In chapter 5 we shall discuss the single transferable vote.

The Working of the German Electoral System

The German electoral system was adopted by the Federal Republic of Germany which, established in 1949, faced the problem of constructing a new democracy on very unsure foundations. For Germany's first experiment in democracy – the Weimar Republic, which lasted from 1919 to 1933 – failed to take root among the German people and was overthrown by Hitler. Elections in the Weimar Republic were conducted under a system of proportional representation which maximized the opportunities for small parties and gave the German elector little personal contact with his MP. This electoral system was blamed – probably unfairly – for the downfall of the Weimar Republic, and the post-war constitution-makers were anxious to avoid the mistakes of their predecessors.

The founders of the Federal Republic decided not to abandon proportional representation, despite the unfortunate experience of the Weimar Republic. Instead they tried to devise a proportional system which would mitigate the evils of the system used in Germany in the 1920s, maintain a personal link between the MP and his constituents, yield stable government, yet also provide a legislature in which the allocation of seats accurately reflected the number of votes

Voting Slip

for the Parliamentary Election in the Constituency of (63)Bonn on 6 March 1983

You Have 2 Votes

1 Vote Here for the election of a **Constituency Representative** (first vote)	1 Vote Here for the election of a **Regional List (Party)** (second vote)

1	**Prof. Dr Ehmke,** Horst			SPD	Sozialdemokratische Partei Deutschlands	1
	Professor für öffentliches Recht Bonn Am Römerlager 4	**SPD**	Sozialdemokratische Partei Deutschlands		Brandt, Wischnewski, Frau Huber, Schmidt, Frau Renger	

1 Prof. Dr Ehmke, Horst
Professor für öffentliches Recht, Bonn, Am Römerlager 4 — **SPD** — Sozialdemokratische Partei Deutschlands

2 Dr Daniels, Hans
Notar, Bonn, Schmidbonnstr. 7 — **CDU** — Christlich Demokratische Union Deutschlands

3 Rentrop, Franz Friedheim
Steuerberater u. Wirtschaftsprüfer, Bonn-Bad Godesberg, Langenbergsweg 72 — **F.D.P.** — Freie Demokratische Partei

4 Rohde, Volker August Wilhelm Fritz
Journalist, Bonn-Beuel, Stroofstr. 15 — **DKP** — Deutsche Kommunistische Partei

5 Dr Skupnik, Wilfried Bruno
Beamter, Bonn, Clausiusstr. 21 — **GRÜNE** — DIE GRÜNEN

Regional List (second vote):

1 SPD Sozialdemokratische Partei Deutschlands — Brandt, Wischnewski, Frau Huber, Schmidt, Frau Renger

2 CDU Christlich Demokratische Union Deutschlands — Dr Barzel, Dr Blüm, Frau Dr Wilms, Vogel, Frau Hürland

3 F.D.P. Freie Demokratische Partei — Genscher, Dr Graf Lambsdorff, Frau Dr Adam-Schwaetzer, Dr Hirsch, Möllemann

4 DKP Deutsche Kommunistische Partei — Mies, Frau Nieth, Frau Bobrzik, Bublitz, Frau Buschmann

5 GRÜNE DIE GRÜNEN — Vogel, Frau Dr Vollmer, Stratmann, Frau Nickels, Schily

6 EAP Europäische Arbeiterpartei — Frau Zepp-La Rouche, Cramer, Frau Cramer, Schiele, Vitt

7 KPD Kommunistische Partei Deutschlands (Marxisten-Lennisten) — Brand, Detjen, Frau Schnoor, Voß, Frau Lenger-Koloska

8 NPD Nationaldemokratische Partei Deutschlands — Schultz, Gerlach, Frau Krüger, Siepmann, Aengenvoort

9 USD Unabhängige Soziale Demokraten — Bönnemann, Vorhagen, Thränhardt, Bartz, Stahlschmidt

FIGURE 2   *Ballot paper used for the parliamentary election in the constituency of Bonn (63) on 6 March 1983*

cast. To achieve these diverse aims, the Federal Republic adopted a system which contains elements of the British electoral system but modified so as to secure proportionality.

The German voter is faced with a ballot paper of the type shown in figure 2. He has two votes, the first being for a constituency representative, as in Britain, while the second half is a vote for a party. The voter is under no obligation to cast his second vote for the same party as the constituency candidate for whom he has cast his first vote. If, for example, he casts his first vote for Dr Daniels, the Christian Democrat candidate, he can decide to cast his second vote not for the CDU but, say, for the Free Democrats (FDP). Indeed, as we shall see, it can be a perfectly rational strategy for the voter to split his two votes in this way.

When the votes are counted, constituency representatives are elected from the total of first votes, as in Britain. The candidate with the most first votes in each constituency, whether or not he has an absolute majority, becomes a member of the legislature. But – and here the system diverges from that used in Britain – the constituency representatives fill only half (248) of the 496 seats in the German lower house, the Bundestag. The other 248 seats are filled so as to ensure that the number of seats allocated to each party is proportional to the votes cast for them. This is done by first computing how many seats each party would be entitled to on a strictly proportional basis and then *subtracting* from these totals the number of seats which each party has won in the constituency contests. The figure remaining is the total number of extra seats which each party is entitled to receive on the basis of its second votes.

There is just one qualification to be made, however. For under the German system a party which fails to secure at least 5 per cent of the vote across the country as a whole, or three constituency seats, cannot take part in the allocation of seats based on second votes. This provision was introduced to prevent the system from being made unworkable – as many claimed the Weimar Republic had been – by the growth of small, extremist parties which could paralyse the business of government.

The working of the German system can be illustrated by examining the results of an actual election, that held in March 1983. The result in terms of first votes was as follows:

	% votes	No. of seats
Christian Democrats	52.1	180
Social Democrats	40.4	68
Free Democrats	2.8	—
Greens (an ecology party)	4.1	—

When the total of the second votes were counted, however, the proportion of the vote which each party received was as follows:

Christian Democrats	48.8%
Social Democrats	38.2%
Free Democrats	6.9%
Greens	5.6%

No other party managed to win 5 per cent of the total vote.

When the votes of parties failing to win 5 per cent of the total vote had been excluded, the total number of seats to which each of the remaining parties was entitled was as follows:

Christian Democrats	244 seats
Social Democrats	191 seats
Free Democrats	34 seats
Greens	27 seats

The number of constituency seats which each party had won was then subtracted from the total number of seats to which it was entitled, using the criterion of proportionality. The result gave the number of additional members to which each party was entitled. The Christian Democrats were entitled to 244 minus 180 members (i.e. 64 extra members); the Social Democrats to 191 minus 68 (i.e. 123 extra members). As for the Free Democrats and the Greens, since they had won no constituency seats at all, all of their members were additional members.

But how are these non-constituency members chosen? They derive from a party list which is presented to the electorate by each party on a regional basis. The list is an ordered one, on which candidates are numbered to indicate their position in the order. In figure 2 the names of the leading figures on the list can be found in the right-hand column under the name of the party to which they belong. Thus the Social Democrats' list is headed in this particular region by Brandt, Wischnewski, Frau Huber, Schmidt and Frau Renger, while the Christian Democrats' list is headed by Dr Barzel, Dr Blüm, Frau Dr Wilms, Vogel and Frau Hürland.

The number of seats to which each party is entitled from the list is, as we saw above, Christian Democrats 64, Social Democrats 123, Free Democrats 34 and Greens 27. This means that the first 64 on the various regional lists of the Christian Democrats are elected, the 64 being taken from each region in proportion to the total Christian Democrat vote in that region. Similarly, the first 123 on the Social Democrats' lists are elected, the first 34 on the Free Democrats' list and the first 27 on the Greens' list.

There are no by-elections under the German electoral system. If a member of the Bundestag resigns or dies, his seat is filled, whether the member concerned was a constituency member or a list member, by inviting the next available candidate on the list to take his place. This means, of course, that it is not possible for the German elector to indicate his dissatisfaction with a Government in mid-term, as in Britain. However, Germany has a well developed structure of regional government, and elections to the regional authorities, which take place on a different cycle from those of the central government, play a similar role in Germany to by-elections in Britain, in that they are used as a barometer of public attitudes towards central government.

There is just one further minor complication to deal with before we can conclude our description of the West German electoral system. It does happen, very occasionally, that a party wins more seats from its *first* vote – its constituency result – than its total entitlement under its *second* vote, the proportional representation vote. When this happens, the party is allowed to retain its extra seats, and the size of the Bundestag is enlarged. The number of extra seats has never, in any election, exceeded five. In the 1983 election there were just two such excess seats, both of which were won by the Social Democrats in their strongholds of Hamburg and Bremen. This meant that instead of the 191 members to which the Social Democrats were strictly entitled, they gained 193 seats, and the size of the Bundestag was enlarged from 496 to 498 seats. Thus the final result of the election was:

Christian Democrats	244 seats
Social Democrats	193 seats
Free Democrats	34 seats
Greens	27 seats
Total	498 seats

It will be seen that no party enjoys an absolute majority of seats, the Christian Democrats being just five seats short of 50 per cent of the seats, 249. Since October 1982, however, the Christian Democrats and the Free Democrats had governed together as a coalition, and both parties had gone to the electorate on a coalition programme. The Christian Democrat/Free Democrat coalition commanded, as a result of the election, a comfortable majority in the Bundestag, with 278 seats out of 498.

The German electoral system combines a single-member constituency system of the British type with proportional representation. It is because it retains the single-member constituency that this system has proved so attractive to many supporters of proportional representation in Britain. Of course, the introduction of the German system into Britain would mean that only 50 per cent of the MPs would be elected from the constituencies, the other 50 per cent being chosen from party lists. Thus either the House of Commons would have to be doubled to 1,300 members or – and this, of course, is by far the more likely solution – constituencies would have to be doubled in size so that there would be only 325 constituency MPs. Thus the average parliamentary constituency in Britain would comprise an electorate not of about 65,000 as at present but of about 130,000.

The German electoral system is highly proportional but not totally so, since the 5 per cent threshold excludes small parties. This means that large parties come to be slightly over-represented. The degree of over-representation, however, is nowhere near as large as under the British electoral system or under the alternative vote or two-ballot systems:

	% votes	% seats
Christian Democrats	48.8	49.0
Social Democrats	38.2	38.8
Free Democrats	6.9	6.8
Greens	5.6	5.4
Others	0.5	0.0
Total	100.0	100.0

Turnout is comparatively high in Germany. Since 1953 it has been well over 80 per cent, while in 1972 and 1976, it was over 90 per cent. In the last two elections, those in 1980 and 1983, turnout was 89.1 and 88.6 per cent respectively. We may compare these figures with their British equivalents. Since 1955 turnout in British general elections has never reached 80 per cent and in the last two elections, in 1979 and 1983, it was 76 and 72.6 per cent respectively. To the extent that turnout is a measure of electoral satisfaction, it can at least be said that Germans display a high degree of contentment with their electoral system. Moreover, thanks to the second vote – the proportional vote – every vote cast, even in a constituency which is safe for one party, counts towards the total and assists towards the election of a member of the Bundestag. In Britain, by contrast, only votes cast for winning candidates actually help to elect a Member of the House of Commons. Votes cast for other candidates have no effect and make no contribution to the outcome.

As can be seen from the results of the 1983 election, proportional representation in Germany has not led to a multiplicity of parties or to the growth of extremist parties. On the contrary, the 5 per cent threshold which parties must surmount to secure representation has served progressively to exclude small parties from the Bundestag. In the first elections held in 1949, shortly after the birth of the Federal Republic, there were no fewer than 10 parties in the Bundestag. By 1961, however, only three were able to secure representation – the Christian Democrats, the Social Democrats and the Free Democrats; and no party, once excluded from the Bundestag, has yet succeeded in resuming its representation there. In 1983 the two major parties, the Christian Democrats and the Social Democrats, secured 87 per cent of the second votes between them as compared with the 70 per cent of the vote gained by the British Labour and Conservative parties in the 1983 general election.

From 1961 to 1983 there remained just three parties in the Bundestag, but in 1983 they were joined by the Greens, who were able to capitalize upon the widespread anxiety felt at the stationing of American cruise missles in Germany. Neverthe-less, the number of parties now in the Bundestag, four, is smaller than the 10 returned in Britain's general election in 1983; and whereas the number of parties able to win seats in Germany has *decreased* since 1949, in Britain the number of parties in the Commons has *increased* from three in 1950 to 10 in 1983.

Of course, all but one of these new parties – the SDP is the exception – are regional parties: the Scottish and Welsh Nationalists and four Northern Ireland parties. This means that if it were to be adopted in Britain, the German electoral system would have to be modified so that the 5 per cent threshold applied not to the country as a whole but to each region. Thus, to secure representation in the Commons in a particular region, a party would have to win 5 per cent of the vote in that region. A national threshold of 5 per cent would be unfair to those parties such as the Scottish and Welsh Nationalists and the Northern Ireland parties which choose to compete electorally only in one part of the country.

Still, there is no reason why a proportional system of the German type should encourage fragmentation of parties or the growth of new parties. If introduced in Britain, the German system would alter the relative strengths of the existing parties, but it would be unlikely to stimulate the growth of new ones.

Two Classes of MP?

In order to combine the single-member constituency with proportional representation, the German electoral system provides for two classes of MP, and this, of course, would be novel and unfamiliar to the British voter. It would be natural to expect, in the British context, that MPs elected from the list would be treated as second-class MPs by their colleagues elected by constituencies, since the list Members would not have won their seats by putting themselves directly before the electorate. But in the Federal Republic this kind of discrimination does not occur. Whether an MP comes from a constituency or a list seems entirely irrelevant to his standing in the Bundestag.

This may, however, be due to factors peculiar to Germany which would not necessarily apply in Britain. Since 1961 only the Christian Democrats and the Social Democrats have been able to win constituency seats: The Free Democrats (and in 1983 the Greens) have won all their seats from the list. When party leaders such as Hans-Dietrich Genscher, currently the leader of the Free Democrats, and Walter Scheel, the former leader, are elected from the list, it becomes difficult to regard such MPs as second-class. Further, Willy Brandt, who was the Federal German Chancellor from 1969 to 1974, was also a candidate elected from the list and did not put himself forward for any constituency. However, most list candidates (around 95 per cent) put themselves forward in constituencies as well, regarding their place on the list as insurance in case they fail in the constituency.

Since West Germany is a federal state, constituency members necessarily play a smaller role in dealing with grievances than in Britain, a unitary and highly centralized country. A German who has a complaint about the operation of the public authorities is far more likely to be directed to his regional or local government than to his Bundestag member, whose function is primarily to scrutinize federal legislation.

It does not follow, of course, that a system which operates perfectly satisfactorily in Germany could command similar acceptance in Britain, since notions of the proper role of the MP differ very considerably in the two countries. The question at issue for the British voter is whether the quality of representation will suffer if Westminster constituencies are doubled in size. That is a question which we shall consider in the context of the single transferable vote, in chapter 5, since that particular system would necessitate even larger constituencies than the German system requires. We shall find, however, that there are some myths which need to be cleared away before we can properly assess the nature of the MP–constituent relationship.

A further objection to the German system is that a candidate rejected by his constituency can still enter the Bundestag through the party list, so that the list can help to protect unpopular candidates from the electorate. Is it not profoundly undemocratic that Members should be elected, even if they have little popular support, just because they happen to enjoy the confidence of their party organization?

To some extent, the German electoral law manages to counter this objection by requiring that the party lists be chosen by a democratic procedure. One way of meeting this requirement would be to hold primary elections, as in the United States; in the Federal Republic, however, most list candidates are chosen by secret ballot at a duly constituted party convention. This means that not all party members are directly involved in choosing the list candidates, but only the party activists who become delegates at the convention. In theory, such a method of selection could lead to undistinguished or unrepresentative candidates being given high places on the list. But it is fair to say that few such complaints are to be heard in Germany, where the quality of members of the Bundestag is considered very high. Nevertheless, the German electoral system must carry with it the danger that it yields too much power to the party machine unless candidates on the list are chosen through an open procedure such as a party primary.

If the German electoral system were to be introduced in Britain, and the parties were required to hold primaries, the law would have to involve itself in the internal workings of the political parties to ensure that the primaries were held fairly and that they were confined to duly registered party members. Decisions would have to be made about whether the proper procedures had been complied with. Where difficulties arose the courts could be called upon to settle disputes.

This would be a considerable innovation for Britain, since at present the law has little to do with the internal workings of the parties, which are regulated largely by informal conventions rather than by statute.

Primary elections would also require the parties to formalize their membership arrangements so that they could determine who precisely was entitled to vote in a primary election. At present the membership arrangements of the parties, particularly those of the Conservatives and Liberals, are rather loose, and the two parties are unable to provide any exact indication of membership figures. It may be argued that it is all to the good that such loose arrangements come to be superseded by more formal practices, but there are many who would see such a change as a departure from the long-established convention that, the parties being voluntary organizations, their internal operations should not be the concern of the law. The tacit understandings which regulate British and German attitudes to political parties are, in fact, very different, a product no doubt of the different histories of the two countries. Britain is a country in which democracy has come about through an evolutionary process, and there is considerable confidence in the ability of the parties to manage their own affairs. In Germany, on the other hand, it was difficult, after the experience of Hitler, to place much confidence in the working of institutions unless these were closely regulated by statute law. There would therefore be difficulties in transferring the German system to Britain – although, of course, there is no reason to believe that these difficulties could not be overcome.

The German Party System

The three main parties in Germany, the Christian Democrats, Social Democrats and Free Democrats, correspond in a very rough way to the three main parties in Britain, Conservative, Labour and Liberals. Yet the workings of the party system in Germany diverge very considerably from the British model because of Germany's proportional electoral system.

The essence of a system of proportional representaiton is that no party can secure an absolute majority in the legislature unless it gains 50 per cent of the vote. In Germany, however, an absolute majority can be secured on a little less than 50 per cent of the vote, since, as we have seen, large parties come to be slightly over-represented in the system, a result of the elimination of small parties by means of the 5 per cent threshold, the only deviation in the German system from the rule of strict proportionality.

As absolute majority of seats has only once been secured in Germany, in 1957, by the Christian Democrats who nevertheless decided to govern in coalition with two small parties electorally dependent upon them. But after every other election coalition government has been inevitable in Germany if majority government is to be secured.

There have been twelve Governments in Germany since 1949:

* 1949   Christian Democrat/Free Democrat coalition with smaller parties
* 1953   Christian Democrat/Free Democrat coalition with smaller parties
* 1957   Christian Democrat coalition with smaller parties
* 1961   Christian Democrat/Free Democrat coalition
* 1965   Christian Democrat/Free Democrat coalition
  1966   Christian Democrat/Social Democrat coalition –the Grand Coalition
* 1969   Social Democrat/Free Democrat coalition
* 1972   Social Democrat/Free Democrat coalition
* 1976   Social Democrat/Free Democrat coalition
* 1980   Social Democrat/Free Democrat coalition
  1982   Christian Democrat/Free Democrat coalition
* 1983   Christian Democrat/Free Democrat coalition

Note: * denotes general election year.

One obvious feature of German government is immediately apparent from the above list – the pivotal role played by the Free Democrats. The Free Democrats are the only one of the three major parties which can form a coalition with either of the other two. For this reason, it has enjoyed a share in govern-

TABLE 4   *The share of the vote of the three main German parties since 1969 (%)*

Year	Christian Democrats	Free Democrats	Social Democrats
1969	46.1	5.8	42.7
1972	44.9	8.4	45.8
1976	48.6	7.9	42.6
1980	44.5	10.6	42.9
1983	48.8	6.9	38.2

ment since the Republic was founded in 1949 except for two periods: 1957 to 1961, when the Christian Democrats, having an overall majority in the Bundestag, did not need them; and the years of the Grand Coalition, 1966 to 1969.

This pivotal role can be seen even more clearly if we look at table 4. It will be seen that the Free Democrats have failed to secure more than one-tenth of the vote since 1969. Their share of the vote, in fact, has been lower than that of the British Liberals (and the Liberal/SDP Alliance) in the last four elections:

1974 (February)	19.3%
1974 (October)	18.3%
1979	13.8%
1983	25.4%

Yet the Free Democrats have been in government continuously since 1969, while the British Liberals have not been able to wield any influence on government at all – except perhaps during the seventeen months of the Lib-Lab pact with James Callaghan's Labour Government in 1977–8.

Not only have the Free Democrats been in government for the whole of the period since 1969; they have also been able to determine which of the other two parties is in government with them. As table 4 shows, the Christian Democrats have gained more support than the Social Democrats in every German election since 1969 except that of 1972; yet from 1969 to 1982 Germany was governed not by the Christian Democrats and the Free Democrats but by the Social Democrats and Free Democrats. The Christian Democrats were denied office because the Free Democrats found the Social Democrat party a more congenial coalition partner. The Free Democrats were thus able to decide, with 10 per cent of the vote or less, which of the two major parties, each of whom had been able to win four times as many votes, should form a Government.

During the 1970s the Christian Democrats were unable to enter government, although in 1976 they nearly gained an absolute majority of seats in the Bundestag and managed to secure a greater share of the vote than any British party has received since 1959. Unless the Christian Democrats were able to gain an absolute majority in the Bundestag, their only hope of entering government was to wean the Free Democrats away from their alliance with the Social Democrats, and the Christian Democrats bent all their efforts to this aim, which was finally achieved in October 1982.

Thus within quite broad limits the German party system remains impervious to gains or losses by the two major parties. What counts for these parties is not so much the size of their vote but whether they are acceptable to the Free Democrats as coalition partners. In October 1982 the Government of Germany changed not so much because there was a radical change in the opinion of the German electorate but because the Free Democrats decided to exchange coalition partners. Indeed, there has been no complete change of Government personnel, as regularly occurs in Britain, since the founding of the Federal Republic. Each time there has been a major change of Government – 1966, 1969 and 1982 – it has come about through a change of coalition partners. In 1966 the Christian Democrat/Free Democrat coalition was superseded by a Grand Coalition of Christian Democrats and Social Democrats; in 1969 this Government, in turn, was replaced by a new coalition of Social Democrats and Free Democrats which lasted until 1982, when it was supplanted by a Government of Christian Democrats and Free Democrats.

It is this feature of the German system – and it is paralleled in other proportional systems – which gives rise to objections on the part of those who dislike proportional representation. The German electoral system, such critics suggest, only *seems* to offer better representation than the British. In fact, it offers worse representation for two reasons. The first is the excessive influence it gives to a pivot party of the centre such as the Free Democrats. The German system of proportional representation gives the Free Democrats disproportional representation in government. There is no reason to believe that this is what the electorate wants. A majority of the voters support the Christian

Democrats or the Social Democrats, but a coalition with the Free Democrats means that the distinctive policies of neither major party can be carried out.

Secondly, the critics argue that the German system allows the voter less representation than the British because coalition government is itself less representative than single-party government, since coalitions are formed not by the voter but by the party leaders in their famous 'smoke-filled rooms'. Governments are formed not through the electoral process but through a process which begins only when all the votes have been counted. This gives greater power to the party leaders, who become skilled horse-traders of coalition policies, but less power to the voter, who has little say in the formation of coalitions or the agreements which underpin them.

These criticisms of the German system are not, however, quite as powerful as they may seem. They rest upon the premise that the voter has no say at all in the question of which parties should form a coalition government. But this is unlikely to be correct. For no party in a democracy, when negotiating with others on the formation of a coalition, is able to ignore the wishes of those who vote for it. If it does so, the party will lose electoral support. When in 1969 the Free Democrats decided to support the Social Democrats rather than the Christian Democrats, whom they had supported since 1966, they lost a good many of their supporters on the right and only just succeeded in surmounting the 5 per cent threshold. Similarly when in 1982 the Free Democrats decided to switch their support from the Social Democrats to the Christian Democrats, so causing the fall of Helmut Schmidt's Government and its replacement with one led by Helmut Kohl, they had to face a number of resignations from their more left-wing members, including the General Secretary of the party.

There was talk of a breakaway Liberal party of the left being formed, and many observers again doubted whether the Free Democrats would be able to surmount the 5 per cent threshold in the elections of 1983, whose function it was to endorse or reject the new coalition. In the event these fears were not realized, but the dangers involved in changing coalition partners, when such a course is not favoured by a party's supporters or by opinion in the country, are clear. No party would undertake such a decision lightly.

Moreover, the German system, because it provides for two votes – a constituency vote and a party vote – allows the voter to endorse or reject a proposed coalition. By convention, the parties announce their intentions with respect to coalition formation before the election takes place. In 1983 the Free Democrats and Christian Democrats made it clear to the electorate that they proposed to continue their coalition, while in 1972, 1976 and 1980 the Free Democrats and Social Democrats left no one in any doubt that they would maintain their coalition if the voters endorsed it. Thus voters know, before they cast their ballots, that two parties are in coalition, and they can vote for or against it.

The German electoral system offers voters a further opportunity to indicate their view of a proposed coalition arrangement: they can, if they wish, split their votes, giving their constituency vote to one party and their list vote to another.

As we have seen, the Free Democrats have not won a constituency seat since 1957. All their seats, therefore, come from the second, list vote. A constituency vote for the Free Democrats is likely to be a wasted vote. This means that voters who wish to support the Free Democrats might well consider it worth while to use their first votes for whichever of the two major parties they most favour. If they favour a coalition with the Social Democrats, they can use their first vote for the Social Democrat constituency candidate; if the Christian Democrats, they can vote for the Christian Democrat candidate. In this way the voter can indicate the type of coalition which he or she favours.

Moreover, in some recent general elections in Germany, as we have noted, the Free Democrats have been in danger of falling below the 5 per cent threshold. Therefore in 1972 and 1976 Social Democrats might well have felt justified in using their second vote for the Free Democrat list in order to help that party surmount the threshold. Finally, supporters of the Social Democrats or Christian Democrats might well prefer that their party be without an absolute majority in the Bundestag so that it cannot implement its more doctrinaire policies. This constitutes another reason for vote-splitting, for supporting one of the major parties on the first ballot and the Free Democrats on the second. Such vote-splitting offers an insurance against both the left wing of the Social Democrats and the right wing of the Christian Democrats, since if the major parties cannot secure a majority, they will have to co-operate with their coalition partners, the Free Democrats, and their more extreme policies will have to be abandoned.

The possibility of vote-splitting, therefore, allows the voter to endorse or reject a particular coalition arrangement. We can see it in operation in the 1960s when the Free Democrats shifted from support of the Christian Democrats in the election of 1965 to the Social Democrats in the election of 1969. Table 5 shows the *constituency* votes cast by those

TABLE 5 *Constituency votes of Free Democrat list voters*

Party	1965	1969
Social Democrats	6.7	24.8
Christian Democrats	20.9	10.6
Free Democrats	70.3	62.0
Others/invalid votes	2.1	2.6

whose list votes were for the Free Democrats in 1965 and 1969. On each occasion the majority of Free Democrat voters also supported a Free Democrat constituency candidate – but without effect, since the Free Democrats did not win a single constituency seat in either election. But in 1965 two-thirds of those Free Democrat voters who did *not* vote a straight ticket supported the Christian Democrats; while in 1969 nearly two-thirds of Free Democrat voters who did not vote a straight ticket supported a Social Democrat constituency candidate. This shows, surely, that a majority (though not, of course all) of the Free Democrat voters approved of the party's switch of coalition partners.

In 1972, as the figures below show, a majority of Free Democrats actually used their first votes to support the Social Democrats. This was in response to appeals by the Social Democrat and Free Democrat leaders to use their votes so as to give maximum support to the coalition. The constituency votes of those whose second (list) votes were for the Free Democrats in 1972 were as follows:

Social Democrats	52.9%
Christian Democrats	7.9%
Free Democrats	38.2%
others/invalid votes	1.0%

By the time of the 1983 election the Free Democrats had changed sides again. As we saw on p. 51, the Free Democrats did much better on the second vote than on the first. Had they not done so, they would have failed to secure representation in the Bundestag, since their first (constituency) vote was only 2.8 per cent. The distribution of Free Democrat list votes to constituency candidates was as follows:

Social Democrats	10.1%
Christian Democrats	58.3%
Free Democrats	29.1%
Others/invalid votes	2.5%

Clearly, the majority of Free Democrat list voters did not wish to waste their first votes; and perhaps some Christian Democrats used their second vote for the Free Democrats so that Helmut Kohl would fail to win an absolute majority and thus be compelled to move towards the centre in coalition with the Free Democrats. The distribution of Free Democrat list votes shows that a majority who supported the party also favoured the idea of co-operation with the Christian Democrats.

The German system, it is clear, exerts a centripetal pull upon the parties, steering them towards a consensus position. A political leader who takes a firm left- or right-wing view is likely to prove unacceptable because he will not be able to secure the support of the Free Democrats which has proved so essential for Government formation.

That is one reason why a politician of the right such as Franz-Josef Strauss has been unable to achieve power; and also why the German Social Democrats are so far to the right of the British Labour Party. Indeed, in 1959 the Social Democrats decided to jettison their commitment to public ownership and to socialism so as to become a modern party of the moderate Left. By 1972, the party's election slogans indicated how far it had travelled along that particular road: 'Germans, we can be proud of our country'; 'Property owners, you can be proud of your property.'*

The German political parties are closer to the centre than their British counterparts. Indeed, they crowd the centre ground, while there remains little space for radical alternatives. Critics of proportional representation sometimes maintain that it encourages extremism, but that can hardly be said of the German electoral system. Indeed, the danger is the opposite —not extremism but complacency and perhaps political stagnation.

In the Federal Republic a much narrower range of political opinion is given expression than in Britain. It may be that viewpoints which challenge the status quo fail to receive sufficient attention — valuable new ideas may fail to get a hearing, and a consensus which has failed will not be properly challenged. This is a consequence of Germany's troubled past as well as of her electoral system; it is the inevitable disadvantage of a system which encourages consensus politics.

It is this pressure toward the adoption of consensus politics

* Tony Burkett, *Parties and Elections in West Germany: The Search for Stability* (London, Hurst, 1975), p. 123.

which supporters of proportional representation in Britain admire, and they believe that Britain would be better governed if, instead of sharp swings between left and right, there was more agreement on the fundamental principles by which a modern industrial society should be run. But the opponents of proportional representation question the value of such a consensus. It would exclude from Britain's political life leaders of the type whom Mrs Thatcher has called 'conviction politicians'. The German system would make it, if not impossible, at least very difficult to secure that radical reappraisal of policies which, from their very different perspectives, both Mrs Thatcher's Conservatives and the Labour left seek. That consideration provides for some a convincing argument against proportional representation, while to others it constitutes a strong case for it.

The Hansard Society's System

The central difficulty which faces advocates of proportional representation who would like to see the adoption of the German system in Britain lies in the notion of the party list. Whatever assurances are given with regard to the democratic selection of candidates, many people in Britain would find it difficult to support a system which allowed candidates to be elected to Parliament simply because they happen to be nominated by their party. Admittedly, in Britain selection for a safe seat is almost the equivalent. To be chosen as a Conservative candidate for Bournemouth or Labour candidate for Hull offers just the same certainty of election as a high place on the party list in Germany, but at least selection for parliamentary seats is carried out by local constituency organizations and not by the central party machine. Britain, in contrast to Germany, does not have well developed regional party organizations, and it could well be the national party organizations rather than the regional ones which made up the party list. There would always be the fear that the list would be used by the parties to reward loyal apparatchiks on whose vote they could always rely. Such a process would encourage conformity and discourage independence of mind. It would make party discipline in the Commons too strict and would render the MP far too dependent upon the favour of his party for his seat in Parliament.

It is to meet such criticisms that a variant of the German system has been suggested for Britain. This variant was first proposed by a highly prestigious independent Commission set up by the Hansard Society for Parliamentary Government. The Commission was chaired by Lord Blake, the distinguished historian and Conservative peer, and among its other members were Sir Jack Callard, a former chairman of ICI, Professor Ralf Dahrendorf, the Director of the London School of Economics and Mr Gwyn Morgan, a former Assistant General Secretary of the Labour Party. The Commission issued its report in June 1976 and laid down a number of criteria which, in its view, a proportional electoral system for Britain ought to meet. The most important of these, for our present purpose, was that 'All candidates should stand in constituency elections, thus submitting themselves to the verdict of the voter.'* This meant, of course, the abolition of the party list. How, then, was proportionality to be secured without a list?

The Commission decided upon the following solution. The House of Commons should remain at roughly its present size – in fact, it should be reduced to 640 members. But of the 640 MPs only three-quarters of these, 480, would be elected in single-member constituencies. This would mean that the size of constituencies would have to be enlarged by one-third, so that the average size of a constituency would be not about 65,000 but about 86,666. The constituencies would still be smaller than under the German system, which would require a doubling of constituency size.

The remaining seats – 160, one-quarter of the Commons – would be allocated to the 'best losers' among defeated

---

* *The Report of the Hansard Society Commission on Electoral Reform*, June 1976, para. 111c.

candidates. This would be done on a regional basis. In each region of the country, each party's candidates who failed to secure election as constituency MPs would be placed in order according to the percentage of the vote which they gained in their constituencies. The additional seats won by each party would then be allocated not to those on a separate party list, as in West Germany, but to the best-placed candidates who had not secured direct election. There would, as in the German system, be a 5 per cent threshold, but it would be a regional one, so that any party which failed to receive 5 per cent of the vote in a particular region would not be entitled to any additional members.

Let us illustrate how this system might work in practice, using as our 'region' Scotland in the 1983 general election. Let us assume that Scotland retained its 72 parliamentary seats. Under the Hansard Society's scheme there would be only 54 constituencies, and the remaining 18 places would be filled by the 'best losers' so as to secure proportionality. In the 1983 general election the percentage vote for the four main political groupings was as follows:

Labour	35.0%
Conservative	28.3%
Alliance	24.5%
Scottish National Party	11.8%

Let us assume, remembering that the British electoral system tends to over-represent the leading party and to under-represent minor parties, that out of the 54 constituency seats each party won the following number of seats:

Labour	25 seats
Conservatives	18 seats
Alliance	9 seats
Scottish National Party	2 seats

However, the proportional share of the total of 72 seats which each party ought to receive would be:

Labour	25 seats
Conservatives	20 seats
Alliance	18 seats
Scottish National Party	9 seats

This means that each party would be entitled to the following number of additional members:

Labour	0 members
Conservatives	2 members
Alliance	9 members
Scottish National Party	7 members

Two additional Conservative members would, therefore, be needed. They would be selected by placing in order, according to their percentage share of the vote, all those Conservative candidates who had failed to secure election as constituency MPs. Then the top two Conservative candidates would become MPs as additional members. A similar procedure would be followed with regard to the 'best losers' from the Alliance and SNP.

The Hansard Society's system* has two main advantages over the German electoral system. The first is that, under the Hansard Society's system, no one can be elected without directly facing the electorate and securing a high percentage of the vote in a constituency, for the Hansard Society's system does away with the need for a party list. It also does away with the need for a second vote. It therefore has the further advantage that the voter is spared the necessity of having to learn a new and unfamiliar voting system. Indeed, there is some reason to believe that even though the German system has been in existence for over thirty years, some voters still do not fully understand it; they believe that the second vote for the party list is a second *preference*, and that is why the Free Democrats receive more support on the second vote than on the first (constituency) vote.† The Hansard Society's system,

* It is, in fact, the electoral system used to elect the regional Parliament in the German province of Baden-Württemberg.

† Burkett, *Parties and Elections in West Germany*, p. 123.

by contrast, does not require any change in the habits of the voter. He has just one vote (a single 'X'), as at present, and can be introduced quite painlessly to the ideas of proportional representation.

The British elector might, however, find it difficult to accustom himself to the idea that a candidate who had *failed* to win a constituency seat should, nevertheless, find himself elected to the Commons, and it could be difficult to convince him of the fairness of such a system. Moreover, under the Hansard Society's system some constituencies would have two. or even three MPs, while others would have only one. The distribution of additional members could seriously affect the relative political strength in the Commons of different areas. It would clearly make a great difference to the pressures which, say, Glasgow could exert in the Commons if most of the Scottish additional members were to come from that city; and if most of the Scottish additional members came from the Scottish Highlands, that too would alter the relative political leverage of different areas on the basis of no discernible principle.

The Hansard Society's system seems to give the voter some influence over which candidates become additional members, but this is deceptive. For a candidate's votes in a single- member constituency are less a measure of his per-sonal popularity than of the popularity of his party in the constituency. An unpopular Conservative will still poll much better in Oxford than in Oldham. The additional members, therefore, would be elected not so much because the voters particularly wanted to be represented by them in the Commons but because the MPs had the good fortune to be selected both for a constituency in which their party polled well and also for a constituency which did not have too many candidates competing for election. For, other things being equal, it would obviously be easier to secure a high share of the vote in a constituency where there were three candidates than one where there were four or five. The system therefore would penalize a candidate who happened to stand in a constituency where a large number of candidates were competing for election.

Indeed, the Hansard Society's system would encourage candidates with no chance of election at all to stand in a constituency so as to boost their party's share of the vote in the region. The National Front, for example, would put up a candidate in every constituency in London in an attempt to surmount the 5 per cent threshold. One consequence of this proliferation of candidates would be that more constituency MPs would be elected on a minority vote and would therefore be less representative of their constituents than they are under the British electoral system.

Finally, the Hansard Society's system would deprive voters of the power which the German system gives them of splitting their votes between a constituency candidate and a party so as to indicate their preferences with regard to coalition formation after the election. The voters, therefore, could no longer signal their desire for a coalition of a particular political colour, and this could be a serious disadvantage in a political system such as Britain's, where proportional representation would almost certainly mean coalition government.

It is highly doubtful whether the compensating advantages of the Hansard Society's system are sufficient to outweigh these defects. This system only apparently does away with the need for a party list; in reality there is a hidden list, which is formed by the 'best losers'. But the composition of this hidden list cannot, by definition, be inspected by the voter before the election. This contrasts markedly with the German system, which at least allows the voter to see the names of the candidates on the list. Under the Hansard Society's proposal there is a list, but it is formed capriciously through the very operations of the first-past-the-post electoral system which advocates of proportional representation criticize. It is difficult to see that it constitutes any improvement upon the German system.

It is the notion of a party list in the German system that is the main stumbling-block for those who might otherwise favour a change in the electoral system, because it could give too much power to the party machine. But the compensating advantages of the German system could be very considerable. It would allow a much more accurate reflection in Parliament of the opinions of the voters than is possible under the British system, and it would ensure that no Government enjoyed an absolute majority in the Commons unless it had secured the support of nearly half the voters. Moreover, the German system gives the voter a great deal of influence over the formation of coalitions. It has been shown to be perfectly compatible with stable and effective government, and there are many who would argue that the electoral system used in Germany, because it makes for stability and moderation, has actually been one of the main causes of that country's economic and social progress.

Let us, however, postpone our verdict on the German electoral system until we have examined its main challenger as the system of proportional representation recommended for Britain by reformers – the single transferable vote.

5

Proportional Legislation: The Single Transferable Vote

The single transferable vote (STV), although like the German system a version of proportional representation, is in most other respects quite different from it. STV was invented in the nineteenth century, apparently by Thomas Wright Hill (1763–1851), the father of Sir Rowland Hill, inventor of the modern postal system. It was elaborated simultaneously in the 1850s by Carl Andrae (1812–93), a Danish mathematician and also Minister of Finance, and by Thomas Hare (1806–91), an English lawyer who in 1859 wrote a *Treatise on the Election of Representatives, Parliamentary and Municipal*, which is still worth reading as an exposition of the defects of the British electoral system and the methods by which Hare proposed to remedy them. Hare succeeded in convincing the political philosopher John Stuart Mill of the merits of his system, and Mill gave it powerful advocacy in chapter 7 of his *Considerations on Representative Government*, published in 1861. From that time until the mid-1970s STV was the favoured system of almost all advocates of proportional representation in Britain.

Indeed, Britain almost came to adopt it after the First World War. In 1917 a Speaker's Conference set up to consider the shape of the post-war electoral system unanimously recommended that proportional representation be adopted for urban constituencies. But this proposal was defeated, ironically as a result of the opposition of Lloyd George, the Prime Minister and Liberal leader, something which he was to regret when the Liberals were reduced to the status of a minor party in the 1920s.

From 1922 proportional representation, using the single transferable vote, became part of the official programme of the Liberal Party, but until the 1970s and the undermining of the two-party system, advocates of proportional representation were to make no headway. However, the increased strength of the Liberal Party and, more recently, the birth of the SDP with its commitment to proportional representation, and the formation of the Alliance have improved the prospects for changing the British electoral system. The Liberals and the SDP decided in the first report of their joint Commission on Constitutional Reform, *Electoral Reform*, published in July 1982, that STV is its favoured system should the Alliance be in a position to form a government.

Although STV has never been used for Westminster elections,* it is nevertheless currently in operation in one part of the United Kingdom, Northern Ireland, for all elections other than Westminster elections. It has been used since 1973 for all local elections in the Province and also to elect the Northern Ireland Assembly, a largely advisory body set up in October 1982. STV is, in fact, the only proportional system to have been used for public elections in the United Kingdom; and it is also regularly employed in various trade union elections, such as those of the National Union of Teachers, and elections to other unofficial bodies, such as the General Dental Council.

Apart from a brief experiment in Denmark in the 1850s, STV has been used only in countries which have at some time been under British rule. It is the 'Anglo-Saxon' method of securing proportional representation. It is employed in the Irish Republic for elections to both Houses of Parliament and in local elections. It is also used to elect the Maltese Parlia-

---

* With the exception of elections to four of the seven university seats between 1918 and 1950.

ment, the Australian upper house, the Senate, and the Tasmanian State Parliament.

STV and Irish Politics

The STV method of proportional representation is a product essentially of mid-Victorian liberalism, whose aim it was to extend the bounds of individual choice. Accordingly, this system, seeks not only to secure proportional representation but also to widen the choice open to the individual elector and, in particular, to allow him to choose between candidates of the same party as well as to choose between parties. In contrast to the German electoral system, it aims to minimize the influence of party in the election of MPs.

STV operates so as to ensure that as many votes as possible are actually used in helping to elect a candidate. Under the British electoral system, by contrast, all votes not cast for the winning candidate are wasted, in the sense that they do not help to elect an MP; while all votes cast for the winning candidate over and above those he needs to secure election are also wasted, in that he could be elected without them. Consider, for example, the result in the Barking constituency in the general election of 1983:

	No. of votes	% vote
Ms J. Richardson (Lab)	14,415	42.1
H. Summerson (Con)	10,389	30.4
J. Gibb (Liberal/Alliance)	8,770	25.6
I. Newport (Independent)	646	1.9

Votes cast for a candidate other than Labour – nearly 58 per cent of the votes cast – were wasted, in that they did not help to elect a candidate; while every Labour vote over and above 10,390 was also wasted, since 10,390 votes would have been sufficient to elect the Labour candidate. Thus the total number of wasted votes was equal to the votes of the Conservative, Liberal/Alliance and Independent candidates (10,389 + 8,770 + 646 = 19,805 votes), together with the surplus Labour votes ($14,415 - 10,390 = 4,025$ votes). Thus the total number of wasted votes is equal to $19,805 + 4,025 = 23,830$, and this amounts to almost 70 per cent of the votes cast in the constituency. STV aims to minimize the wasted vote.

In the above example the surplus votes cast for the Labour candidate in Barking, and all of the votes cast for the Conservatives, Alliance and Independent candidates, might have been of more value if cast in neighbouring constituencies. Perhaps the 4,025 surplus Labour votes could have been used to help another Labour candidate to win the seat in a nearby marginal. Perhaps the Conservative or Alliance votes could have helped Conservative or Alliance candidates to win seats in neighbouring constituencies. We have already seen in our discussion of the British electoral system that the notion of constituency representation – the representation of territory – makes it very difficult to secure proportionality. The system tends to have the consequence that the number of seats a party wins depends not only upon the number of votes which it receives but also upon where these votes are cast.

In order to secure proportionality through STV, we need to construct multi-member constituencies – constituencies returning not one but, say, five members to Westminster. Then votes which, in our example, the Labour candidate does not need because they are surplus can be transferred to other Labour candidates who might be able to make use of them; while Conservative, Alliance and Independent votes can also be transferred if the candidates for whom they were first cast have no chance of winning.

Thomas Wright Hill, the inventor of STV, was a schoolmaster in the Midlands. He used to ask his pupils to elect a committee by standing closest to the boys they liked best. But it would take time for the result to be secured. Some extremely popular boys would have so many other boys standing next to them that they had more support than they needed to secure election, while some less popular boys had so little support that it was clear they could not secure election and that support for them was wasted. The 'voters' would soon appreciate this, of course, and they would move so as to ensure that their 'vote' exerted the maximum effect. It is this principle which STV seeks to put into practice in elections.

The system operates in multi-member constituencies, in which instead of casting an 'X' vote for one candidate as in Britain, the vote is cast preferentially (as with the alternative vote method discussed in chapter 3, although otherwise the two methods have little in common). If a voter's first-preference vote cannot be used to help elect a candidate, either because the candidate for whom the first-preference vote is cast has no chance of election or because the candidate has more votes than he or she needs, then instead of the vote being wasted, it is *transferred* to a second-choice candidate whose election it might help to secure. If it cannot be used for the second-choice candidate, it is again transferred to the third-choice candidate and so on until the vote can be used effectively. Each elector thus has a *single* vote as in the British electoral system, but that single vote, by contrast with the British system, is *transferable* in accordance with the preferences which the elector has marked. The vote can be seen as taking the form of an instruction to the returning officer, directing him to transfer the vote, in accordance with the voter's preferences, so that it can be of maximum use in helping to elect a candidate.

To understand the working of the system it is best to consider an actual example of its use. The example chosen is taken from the last Irish election in November 1982, but before discussing it we must briefly examine the political context within which the election was fought.

There are three main political parties in the Irish Republic: Fianna Fail, Fine Gael and Labour. The Irish Labour Party is roughly equivalent to its British counterpart – although, since it has to operate within a more conservative political culture, it is somewhat to the right of the British Labour Party and, far from being a major party, has always been the weakest of the three. Indeed, it has never secured more than 17 per cent of the vote in any general election, and in the last three elections it has not been able to achieve even 10 per cent of the vote.

Fianna Fail and Fine Gael are divided from each other less by socio-economic issues of the kind which divide Labour from Conservatives than by historical memories. The parties originate from the two factions in the Irish nationalist movement which split in the 1920s over whether or not to accept the treaty with Britain, a split which led to civil war. Fianna Fail was the party of the Irish nationalist leader, Eamon De Valera, and it has generally been the more republican of the two parties. Since 1932 it has been the largest single party in Ireland, and it has been in government for four-fifths of this period.

Fine Gael developed from the grouping which rejected De Valera's uncompromising nationalist claims, and it has remained a less militantly nationalist party than Fianna Fail, although in the past it has been socially more conservative. Under its present leader, Garret FitzGerald, the current Prime Minister of the Irish Republic, however, Fine Gael has developed a social programme of the type more usually propounded by parties of the centre-left. Nevertheless, the differences between the two parties remain bound up with history and family traditions rather than being based on the kinds of issues familiar to the British electorate.

The relationships between the three parties are conditioned by their relative size. Fine Gael can hope to oust Fianna Fail from government only if it can win the support of Labour, and so the real choice for the Irish elector is generally between a single-party Fianna Fail Government or a Fine Gael/Labour coalition. Indeed, on all the occasions since 1932 when Fianna Fail has been in Opposition, the Government has been a coalition formed by Fine Gael and Labour, together (sometimes) with one or two other small parties.

The November 1982 general election came at the end of an unstable period in Irish politics. It was the third general election in a period of 18 months, and it occurred because the Fianna Fail single-party minority Government had been unexpectedly defeated in the Dail (the lower house of the Irish Parliament). The Fianna Fail leader, and Prime Minister until

November 1982, was Charles Haughey, one of the most controversial figures in Irish politics since De Valera, but controversial less because of his policies than because of his flamboyant and – to his enemies – rather devious political style. The Fianna Fail party entered the November 1982 election deeply split between supporters and opponents of Mr Haughey, and this was to affect the results in some constituencies. In the event, Fianna Fail was defeated in the election and Fine Gael and Labour formed a coalition Government which was to enjoy an overall majority in the Dail.

How STV Works

The single transferable vote system requires multi-member constituencies. There are at present 41 such constituencies in the Irish Republic, 13 returning three members, 13 returning four members and the remaining 15 returning five members. The example which we are using to illustrate the working of the system, Carlow–Kilkenny, is a five-member constituency covering two counties of Ireland (see figure 3).

The ballot paper in the Irish Republic is similar to the form used in elections held under the alternative vote system (see figure 1). A vote is cast by marking a '1' by the name of the voter's first preference, a '2' by the name of the second preference, a '3' by the name of the third preference and so on, until the voter has marked all the preferences that he or she wishes.

In the Irish Republic (and in Northern Ireland) the voter is not *required* to indicate more than one preference. A vote is valid so long as there is a '1' placed unambiguously beside the name of a single candidate. However, it is to the voter's advantage to mark all preferences so as to maximize the chance of the vote being used to help elect a candidate. The voter gains nothing from restricting his or her preferences, since later preferences are not considered until earlier ones have been shown to be incapable of helping to elect a candidate; later preferences cannot count against earlier ones.

Carlow–Kilkenny

5 Seats

Quota 9,301

	Aylward* Liam (FF)	Brophy Eileen (Ind)	Crotty* Kieran (FG)	Dowling Dick (FG)	Gibbons* James (FF)	Jones Patrick (Ind)	Lanigan Mick (FF)	Manning Joe (FG)	Meaney Michael (Lab)	Nolan M J (FF)	Pattison* Seamus (Lab)	Slattery Harry (FG)	Walsh Seán (WP)	Non-transferable
1st Count Votes	9,291	1,021	8,377	5,661	7,032	65	1,558	3,436	1,869	6,998	5,642	2,665	2,189	
2nd Count Transfer of Jones's Votes	+6	+18	+2	+3	+6	−65	+8	+4	+1	+8	+2	−	+4	3
Result	9,297	1,039	8,379	5,664	7,038		1,566	3,440	1,870	7,006	5,644	2,665	2,193	
3rd Count Transfer of Brophy's Votes	+39	−1,039	+68	+29	+63		+6	+79	+80	+172	+100	+272	+105	26
Result	9,336		8,447	5,693	7,101		1,572	3,519	1,950	7,178	5,744	2,937	2,298	
4th Count Transfer of Lanigan's Votes			+81	+26	+793		−1,572	+16	+12	+482	+92	+5	+45	20
Result			8,528	5,719	7,894			3,535	1,962	7,660	5,836	2,942	2,343	
5th Count Transfer of Meaney's Votes			+50	+35	+96			+224	−1,962	+317	+1,078	+84	+47	31
Result			8,578	5,754	7,990			3,759		7,977	6,914	3,026	2,390	

6th Count *Transfer of Walsh's Votes*	322	− 2,390	+ 83	+ 945	+ 157		+ 38			+ 363	+ 264	+ 218	
Result			3,109	7,859	8,134		3,797			8,353	8,842	5,972	
7th Count *Transfer of Slattery's Votes*	92		− 3,109	+ 239	+ 256		+ 1,670			+ 54	+ 446	+ 352	
Result				8,098	8,390		5,467			8,407	9,288	6,324	
8th Count *Transfer of Ayward's Surplus*				+ 1	+ 7		+ 3			+ 19	+ 5	−	− 35
Result				8,099	8,397		5,470			8,426	9,293	6,324	
9th Count *Transfer of Manning's Votes*	137			+ 364	+ 421		− 5,470			+ 116	+ 1,912	+ 2,520	
Result				8,463	8,818					8,542	11,205	8,844	
10th Count *Transfer of Crotty's Surplus*	105			+ 105	+ 29					+ 31	− 1,904	+ 1,634	
Result				8,568	8,847					8,573		10,478	
11th Count *Transfer of Dowling's Surplus*				+ 989	+ 93					+ 95		− 1,177	
Result				9,557	8,940					8,668			

FIGURE 3   *The results of the ballot at Carlow-Kilkenny, 1982*
Source: Nealon's Guide to the 24th Dáil and Seanad, 2nd Election 1982, p. 11.

The voting procedure, then, is quite straightforward. The method of counting the votes so as to determine which five candidates are to be elected is a little more complicated. The first step is to work out the minimum number of votes which a candidate needs to be sure of election. This is called the 'electoral quota'. What would the quota be in a five-member constituency such as Carlow–Kilkenny?

At first sight, it might seem as if the quota would be one-fifth of the total vote, but in fact a candidate can win fewer votes than this and still be sure of election. Even if he were to gain only 19 per cent of the votes, for example, he would still be sure of election, since it would be quite impossible for five *other* candidates to secure 19 per cent of the vote. A candidate would be sure of election if he could secure just over one-sixth of the vote, for only when his vote fell to one-sixth would it be possible for five other candidates to secure the same vote. By the same process of reasoning the quota in a four-member seat will be just over one-fifth of the vote and in a three-member seat just over one-quarter. In general the quota will be:

$$\frac{V}{S + 1} + 1$$

where V is the total number of valid votes cast in the election, and S the total number of seats.

In Carlow–Kilkenny the total number of votes cast, which can be computed by adding up the votes in the row at the top marked '1st Count', was 55,804. If we divide this sum by 6 – since the Carlow–Kilkenny is a five-seat constituency – we obtain the figure 9,300 (ignoring fractions). Adding one to this, we get the quota, which is 9,301. Any candidate, therefore, who has succeeded in securing 9,301 is declared elected, since it is impossible for more than five candidates to reach this figure. If we now look at figure 3, it can be seen that no candidate has reached the quota on the first count, although one candidate, Liam Aylward of Fianna Fail, is only 10 votes short of it.

Since no candidate has yet reached the quota, we now eliminate the candidate with the least votes, Jones, and redistribute his votes. This still does not leave any candidate with enough votes to reach the quota, so in the third stage of the count we eliminate the candidate with the least votes, Brophy, and redistribute her votes. Now Aylward has reached his quota and has a surplus of 35 votes more than the quota of 9,301. We could transfer this surplus, but there would be no point in doing so, since it would not help any other candidate attain the quota (Crotty, the next candidate, being nearly 900 votes short).

We therefore continue to eliminate the candidates with the least votes – Lanigan on the fourth count, Meaney on the fifth, Walsh on the sixth and Slattery on the seventh. Aylward's surplus is transferred on the eighth count (although its transfer could still be delayed).

Transferring a surplus is not quite as straightforward as transferring the votes of eliminated candidates, for, of course, the transfer of votes of eliminated candidates includes every one of their votes, whereas for a candidate who has a surplus it is only the surplus which is transferred. But how do we know which votes to transfer?

In the Irish Republic surpluses are transferred in the following manner. All of Aylward's 9,336 votes are sorted into sub-parcels, according to the next available preference recorded on them for candidates who have not been eliminated, and a separate sub-parcel is made of the non-transferable papers (i.e. papers on which no effective subsequent preference is recorded). In fact, there are no non-transferable papers among Aylward's votes.

The proportion of transferable papers in each sub-parcel which is to be transferred is determined by the following formula:

$$\text{Number of votes in sub-parcel } P = \frac{\text{surplus}}{\text{total transferable papers}}$$

Let us assume that 5,070 of Aylward's votes are marked with a second preference for Gibbons. Then Gibbons receives not 5,070 votes but 5,070 votes multiplied by the surplus, which is

35, and divided by the total number of Aylward's transferable papers, which is, in fact, equal to his total vote, i.e. 9,336. The result,

$$5,070 \times \frac{35}{9,336} = 19$$

is the number of votes which is transferred to Gibbons. These transferred votes are taken from the top of the sub-parcel of Aylward's papers which have a second preference for Gibbons. By a similar procedure, five votes are transferred to Crotty, three to Manning, seven to Nolan and one to Pattison.

It might be objected that it could make a difference to the result of the election precisely which 19 votes are taken from Aylward's pile to transfer to Gibbons, since the pattern of later preferences in the 19 votes will depend upon which papers are chosen.

In an election with a total poll of over 55,000 voters the chance that the result will be affected by this procedure is quite remote. Nevertheless, there is a more accurate procedure for transferring surpluses, which is used in electing the Senate of the Irish Republic and also in elections in Northern Ireland where the single transferable vote is used. This method is sometimes known as the 'senatorial rules'. Instead of transferring just the top votes in the sub-parcel, as we did when transferring Aylward's surplus, each transferable vote is given a fractional value, and *all* of the papers in the sub-parcel are transferred to each of the continuing candidates at their reduced, fractional value. Such a method leads to the elimination of the very slight element of chance which exists in the method used to transfer a surplus in Dail elections.

We may now resume our analysis of the count in Carlow – Kilkenny. After the transfer of Aylward's surplus, since no other candidate has reached the quota, we eliminate Manning and transfer his votes. This proves sufficient to bring another candidate, Crotty, above the quota, and he is declared elected. Crotty's surplus is then transferred on the next count, the tenth, and it serves to bring his party colleague, Dowling, beyond the quota. When, on the eleventh count, Dowling's surplus is transferred, Pattison reaches the quota and is declared elected.

There are now only two candidates left in the count, Gibbons and Nolan, competing for the one remaining seat.

TABLE 6   *The November 1982 election in Carlow–Kilkenny*

ELECTED

Liam Aylward (Fianna Fail)	3rd count
Kieran Crotty (Fine Gael)	9th count
Dick Dowling (Fine Gael)	10th count
Seamus Pattison (Labour)	11th count
M. J. Nolan (Fianna Fail)	11th count

VOTING BY PARTY

1st preference	No. of votes	% of votes
Fianna Fail	24,879	44.6
Fine Gael	20,139	36.1
Labour	7,511	13.5
Workers' Party	2,189	3.9
Others	1,086	1.9

STATISTICS

Population	110,626	
Electorate	74,064	
Total poll	56,325	(76.1%)
Spoiled votes	521	(0.7%)
Valid poll	55,804	(75.4%)
Seats	5	
Quota	9,301	
Candidates	13	

SEATS

Fianna Fail	2
Fine Gael	2
Labour	1

Source: Nealon's Guide: 24th Dail and Seanad.

Neither of these two candidates has reached the quota, but clearly further transfers would be pointless. Nolan is therefore declared elected, and Gibbons is the runner-up. At this final stage of the count it is possible to win election without reaching the quota. This is because the 8,668 votes of the runner-up, Gibbons, and the total number of non-transferable votes, 736, which do not help to elect any candidate, themselves total more than a quota.

The count is now complete, and Aylward, Crotty, Dowling, Nolan and Pattison are the elected members for the constituency of Carlow–Kilkenny. The result is shown in table 6.

Is STV too Complicated?

The first reaction of any reader living in Great Britain (though not in Northern Ireland) to the above description is likely to be that it is highly complex and almost impossible to understand. But, in fact, wherever the single transferable vote system is in operation voters find no difficulty in using it to express their preferences. The voter, after all, has to do no more than mark his or her preferences on the ballot paper – an operation far less complicated than filling in the average football pools coupon. Voters need not master the precise details behind the transfer of surplus votes (the most difficult part of the operation of the system to comprehend) provided that they understand the basic principle of the electoral system. There can be no doubt that the Irish voter displays a highly sophisticated grasp of its working. Many voters follow the progress of the count with great interest, and, as we shall see when we come to discuss the political implications of the result in Carlow –Kilkenny, they are able to use their votes to ensure that they secure the kind of representation which they seek.

When STV was introduced for local elections in Northern Ireland in 1973, this had to be done quite hurriedly. There was, however, a short educational campaign of instruction in the new method of voting with the aid of a cartoon character called 'PR Pete' who told the electors, 'PR is as easy as 1, 2, 3. . . .' In the first local authority elections in Northern Ireland only 1.5 per cent of the ballot papers were invalid; in the Irish Republic in November 1982 only 0.74 per cent were invalid. There can be no doubt, therefore, that STV, despite the inevitable complexity of describing it, would cause no problem for the electorate in Great Britain because the principles upon which it is based are entirely clear and logical.

The time taken to complete the count is, of course, longer than in Britain. The process of counting the votes does not begin until the day after the election, and the complete result is not usually known until two days after the election. Of course, the process could be speeded up by the use of a computer,* but this is resisted in Ireland, partly because the Irish voter enjoys the excitement of following the changing fortunes of his favoured candidates.

Political Aspects of STV

We can now return to the result in Carlow–Kilkenny to consider in more detail the working of STV.

The first point to be noted is that a much larger percentage of the votes contribute to the election of a candidate than is possible in a British constituency. Of the 55,804 valid votes cast in the constituency, all but those cast for the runner-up, Gibbons (8,668) and the non-transferable votes (736) – a total of 9,404, about one-sixth of the votes – have been used to elect a candidate. Of those votes which did not help to elect a candidate, the 736 non-transferable votes could not be effective because voters chose not to indicate any further preferences; while those who voted for Gibbons have at least the satisfaction of knowing that two other members of their party, Fianna Fail – Aylward and Nolan – were elected. Each of the three main parties, Fianna Fail, Fine Gael, and Labour,

---

* See D. R. Woodall, 'Computer Counting in STV Elections', *Representation* (the journal of the Electoral Reform Society), vol. 23, no. 90 (Winter 1982/3).

secured representation. Those who supported the small Workers Party, although too few to elect a candidate, nevertheless exerted some influence upon the result and, through their transfer of votes to Labour, helped to elect their next preference. Even those voting for the Independents, who were rapidly eliminated, were able to use their votes effectively in later rounds of the election. In the Irish Republic as a whole 83 per cent of votes cast contributed directly to the election of a candidate. We may contrast this with the situation in Barking (described on p. 77), where nearly 70 per cent of the votes cast *failed* to help elect a candidate.

Moreover, not only have the three major parties won at least one seat in the constituency, but also each party is represented by the candidate or candidates whom the voters most favour. STV, it will be seen, combines a general election, in which there is a choice between parties, with a *primary election*, in which there is a choice between candidates. Moreover, the primary election, which is an intrinsic part of STV, is superior to a separate primary election for two reasons.

The first is that where a separate primary is held, as in the United States, the winner of the primary becomes the party's sole nominee. Supporters of other candidates, therefore, have to vote for a candidate who is not their first preference. Under STV, by contrast, the minority is not disenfranchised. In a multi-member constituency voters can still support a candidate who may not be the first choice of their party and can hope that he may win with the support of uncommitted voters or transfers from candidates of other parties.

Secondly, a primary election is open only to dues-paying or registered party members, and not to the electorate as a whole. Under STV, on the other hand, the primary election is open to every elector who chooses to vote. Instead of going to the expense of organizing a separate primary election, the voter participates in the primary simply by taking part in the election itself.

This element in STV, by which voters can choose between candidates as well as between parties, constitutes one of its most distinctive features and serves to broaden the choice of the elector beyond what is offered to him under either the British or the German electoral systems.

Let us turn again to the Carlow–Kilkenny constituency to see how the voters used the power which STV gives them of choosing between candidates of the same party. Let us look first at the seventh count, the transfer of Slattery's votes. The pattern is shown below:

	No. of votes	% vote
To Fine Gael candidates	2,468	79.4
To Fianna Fail candidates	310	10.0
To Labour candidate	239	7.7
Non-transferable	92	2.9
Total	3,109	100.0

Nearly four-fifths of Slattery's votes went, not surprisingly, to other candidates of his party, Fine Gael. But around two-thirds (1,670) of the 2,468 votes which were transferred to other Fine Gael candidates went to one particular candidate, Manning. Why did so many go to him rather than to Crotty or Dowling, the other Fine Gael candidates left in the count?

The reason is to be found in the territorial allegiance of the various candidates. Carlow–Kilkenny is a two-county constituency, and voters from each county would be anxious to secure the election of a member from their county. Both Slattery and Manning were candidates from Carlow, while Crotty and Dowling were from Kilkenny. It would be natural, therefore, for Fine Gael voters who had supported Slattery to transfer their votes to Manning rather than to Crotty or Dowling.

Of the rest of Slattery's votes 7.7 per cent were transferred to Labour. This is understandable in the light of the fact that if Fine Gael were to form a Government, it could do so only in alliance with Labour. It would therefore be in the interests of a Fine Gael supporter to ensure the election of a Labour candidate rather than one from Fianna Fail, the Opposition party.

What at first sight appears to be strange is that no less than 10 per cent of Slattery's votes went to Fianna Fail candidates, and that of the 310 votes which went to Fianna Fail candidates all but 54 went to Nolan. The reason, again, is a geographical one. Nolan, like Slattery, came from Carlow, while Gibbons, the other Fianna Fail candidate, was from Kilkenny. STV, therefore, allows voters to exercise their choice so as to secure local representation. In this particular example a significant proportion of local voters used their preferences to ensure that they would elect a member from their own locality even if he was from another party, and this played an important role in securing the election of Nolan for the last seat, ahead of Gibbons.

We can see the same pattern at work in the distribution of Manning's votes at the ninth count. The pattern of transfers is as shown below:

	No. of votes	% vote
To Fine Gael candidates	4,432	81.0
To Fianna Fail candidates	537	9.8
To Labour candidate	364	6.7
Non-transferable	137	2.5
Total	5,470	100.0

Here also the vast majority – over four-fifths – of Manning's votes went to other Fine Gael candidates; 364 were transferred to Labour, with whom Fine Gael would have to form a Government if it was to enjoy a majority in the Dail; and of the 537 transfers to the two Fianna Fail candidates 421 went to Nolan who, like Manning, came from Carlow.

In Carlow–Kilkenny there was another way in which voters were able to use the primary mechanism to good effect. Fianna Fail, as we have noticed, was deeply split between supporters of Charles Haughey, the Party leader, and his opponents. Gibbons was a leading opponent of Haughey, while Aylward, Lanigan and Nolan were all supporters. So Fianna Fail voters could indicate their opinion of Haughey's leadership by their pattern of votes and transfers. They could, as it were, 'send a message' to the party and, if they wished, indicate their disapproval of Haughey without voting against their party, something that is not possible under the British electoral system. As it happens, the voters of Carlow–Kilkenny seem to have approved of Haughey, since Gibbons, a former Minister lost his seat. Although Gibbons secured slightly more first-preference votes than Nolan, he was overtaken by Nolan, who benefited both from the pro-Haughey vote and from the votes of those who insisted upon a representative from Carlow.

Gibbons was also overtaken by Seamus Pattison, one of the two Labour candidates whose first-preference vote was almost 1,400 behind Gibbons. Pattison, as we have seen, benefited from transfers not only from his Labour colleague, Meaney, and from the Workers Party candidate, Walsh, but also from Fine Gael, Labour's likely coalition partners. Under STV a candidate such as Pattison, capable of attracting transfers, can defeat a candidate such as Gibbons with a higher first-preference vote but less ability to attract later transfers.

For this reason the system facilitates the formation of coalitions and gives the voter the power to endorse or reject a coalition arrangement proposed by party leaders. In 1973 Fine Gael and Labour formed a 'National Coalition' shortly before the general election, each party recommending its supporters to give their later preferences to the other. This did not occur in November 1982. In fact, Labour had explicitly decided not to enter into any pre-election coalition commitment with Fine Gael. Nevertheless, through the pattern of their transfers, both Labour and Fine Gael voters indicated that they favoured a coalition between their two parties. Had they not done so, the leaders would not have been able to impose a coalition even if they had so wished.

The system, then, facilitates coalition through the operation of inter-party transfers. In Britain if two parties wish to combine, they have to agree upon a reciprocal withdrawal of candidates, otherwise they will split the vote and let in the opposition party. But to reach agreement over which candidates should withdraw in which constituencies can be a highly contentious and complex matter, as the Liberals and SDP found out before the 1983 general election; and after the general election disagreements broke out again about the future of the Alliance, about how candidates were to be selected and about whether there should again be an electoral agreement.

Under STV, by contrast, there would need to be no reciprocal withdrawal by candidates from either of the two parties. Candidates from each party could stand in a multi-member constituency, leaving it to the voters to choose between them. Voters would also be urged to use their later preferences to support the other member of the Alliance. Indeed, the single transferable vote would offer a test of whether voters really wanted the Alliance to continue. For a Liberal or SDP voter who did *not* favour the alliance would simply vote for the candidate of his own party and refuse to transfer to the other party of the Alliance. In this way coalition would come to depend upon the approval or disapproval of the voters, and it would not be possible for the party leaders to impose a coalition against the wishes of the electorate.

Moreover, a coalition Government formed after an election using STV would have more cohesion than one formed under the British electoral system because it would be based upon proven support in the constituencies. Even under the German system parties which work together in coalition – such as the Christian Democrats and the Free Democrats – find themselves competing for the same vote at constituency level. Parties allying in government find themselves enemies in the constituencies, and this can easily breed cynicism and disillusionment with politics. Under STV, on the other hand, allies in government will also be allies in the constituencies. Indeed, they can remain allies in government only as long as they also remain allies in the constituencies.

Is STV Proportional?

In the constituency of Carlow–Kilkenny, as we have seen, the result of the election was that two Fianna Fail members, two

Fine Gael members and one Labour member were returned. The percentage share of first-preference votes as compared with the percentage share of seats was as follows:

	% votes	% seats
Fianna Fail	44.6	40
Fine Gael	36.1	40
Labour	13.5	20
Others	5.8	0
Total	100.0	100.0

It is clear that the result is only very roughly proportional. Fianna Fail is slightly under-represented but would need 60 per cent of the vote to be entitled to a third seat in a strictly proportional eleciton. Both Fine Gael and Labour are slightly over-represented. When we remember that Fine Gael and Labour operate together in government, we can see that the two parties, although they have just 49.6 per cent of the vote between them, have nevertheless won three out of five seats in the constituency. The coalition partners won three-fiiths of the seats for a little under half the vote. The reason for this, of course, is the pattern of inter-party transfers between the two partners. Under STV a party which can attract such transfers will secure more seats on a given first-preference vote than a party which cannot attract transfers.

In the country as a whole the election yielded a result which was very close to proportionality. The main deviation from proportionality was the over-representation of Fine Gael, though this was achieved not at the expense of Fianna Fail but at the cost of the smaller parties and independents.

	% votes	% seats
Fianna Fail	45.2	45.2
Fine Gael	39.2	42.2
Labour	9.4	9.6
Others	6.2	3.0
Total	100.0	100.0

The proportionality of the system derives from the fact that to win a seat a candidate needs to win enough votes to equal a quota. Since each candidate needs one quota to win a seat, the 'cost' of a seat for each candidate in terms of votes should be the same. Thus STV should, in theory, yield perfect proportionality.

In practice, however, as the examples above show, STV departs from full proportionality. There are a number of reasons for this. The first is that, as we have seen in Carlow–Kilkenny, the last member elected in the constituency usually wins without attaining the quota. If candidates elected without reaching the quota are drawn disproportionately from one party, that party will need fewer votes to gain a given number of seats than its opponents and will find itself *over represented*.

Secondly, votes cast for runners-up, such as Gibbons in Carlow–Kilkenny, are wasted in that they have not been used to help elect anyone. If the runners-up are drawn disproportionately from one party, that party will find itself *under-represented* in the legislature.

Finally, the number of votes needed to elect a candidate will vary with constituency size. In a five-member constituency such as Carlow–Kilkenny the quota will be one-sixth of the vote, while in a three-member constituency the quota will be higher – one quarter of the vote. A party which is weak in three-member constituencies will, therefore, find itself *under-represented* as compared with a party which is weak in five-member constituencies.

Parties whose vote is evenly spread and whose candidates cannot reach the quota will also find themselves under-represented. Let us suppose that Britain adopted STV and – an unlikely hypothesis – established three-member constituencies everywhere. Then, in theory, a party could win just under one-quarter of the vote everywhere and fail to win a single seat. If, in such a situation, the Alliance or the Labour vote were to fall below 25 per cent, it would find itself severely under-represented under STV.

Small parties would also find themselves under-represented under STV, as they would under the German system. Indeed, it is more difficult for a small party to win seats in Ireland than in Germany. In Carlow–Kilkenny, for example, a party needs one-sixth of the vote to win a seat, and this is more difficult to achieve than winning 5 per cent of the vote in the country as a whole, which is the requirement in Germany. Between 1965 and 1981 only three parties were represented in the Dail: Fianna Fail, Fine Gael and Labour. In the election of November 1982, however, four out of the 166 members did not owe allegiance to the major parties. There were two independents and two members of a left-wing grouping, the Workers Party, which sought to capitalize on radical discontent with Labour's coalition with 'capitalistic' Fine Gael. In Malta only two parties are represented in Parliament.

The provision made for by-elections in the Irish Republic also allows the Dail to deviate from proportionality between general elections. By-elections are held in the whole constituency, using the alternative vote method described in chapter 3. The effect of this is that if a retiring or deceased Member happens to represent a minority party in the constituency, then that party loses its representation because it is impossible to secure proportionality when there is only one candidate to be elected. Unfortunately, there is no wholly satisfactory method of providing for by-elections either under STV or under any other proportional system.

Because STV deviates from strict proportionality, it can yield anomalous results, in that the party with the most first preference votes may fail to win the most seats. There was a spectacular example in Malta in 1981, when in a two-party system the Nationalists, who won 50.9 per cent of first-preference votes gained fewer seats, 31, than Dom Mintoff's Labour Party, which for 49.1 per cent of first-preference votes was rewarded with 34 seats.

This perverse result seems to have occurred not through the gerrymandering of constituencies but because more of the votes cast for the Nationalists were wasted as compared with votes cast for Labour. Nationalist candidates were runners-up in nine constituencies, while Labour candidates were runners-up in only four. This was the first time such a result had occurred in Malta over a period of 60 years. It is possible only in a country with a small number of constituencies, where electoral competition is confined to two closely matched parties. It would be highly unlikely to occur in a country such as Britain, where many parties compete for election in a large number of constituencies.

But there have also been some highly anomalous results in the

TABLE 7   *General election results in the Irish Republic, 1965, 1969, 1973*

Party	% First-preference votes	% seats	Government
1965			
Fianna Fail	47.7	50.3	Fianna
Fine Gael	34.1	32.9	Fail
Labour	15.4	14.7	
(Fine Gael/Labour)	(49.5)	(47.6)	
Others	2.8	2.1	
1969			
Fianna Fail	45.7	51.7	Fianna
Fine Gael	34.1	35.0	Fail
Labour	17.0	12.6	
(Fine Gael/Labour)	(51.1)	(47.6)	
Others	3.2	0.7	
1973			
Fianna Fail	46.2	47.6	Fine Gael/
Fine Gael	35.1	37.8	Labour
Labour	13.7	13.3	
(Fine Gael/Labour)	(48.8)	(51.1)	
Others	5.0	1.3	

Irish Republic. Consider, for example, the results of the general elections in 1965, 1969 and 1973 (see table 7). In 1965 and 1969 Fianna Fail won an overall majority of the seats in the Dail on less than 50 per cent of the vote. On each occasion it had fewer votes than Fine Gael and Labour combined. Indeed, in 1969 the total votes cast for Fine Gael and Labour together totalled over 50 per cent, yet Fianna Fail, with a smaller share of the vote than in 1965, increased its majority.

In 1973, by contrast, Fianna Fail gained a higher vote than in 1969, and the Fine Gael/Labour total share of the vote was lower than in 1965 or 1969. Yet Fine Gael and Labour won an overall majority of the seats, and Fianna Fail was relegated to the Opposition benches.

One of the reasons for this discrepancy was that in 1973 Fine Gael and Labour fought the election as a 'National Coalition', explicitly calling for inter-party transfers, something which they had not done in 1965 or 1969. These inter-party transfers enabled the two parties to win a greater number of seats for a given share of the vote (as they succeeded in doing in Carlow – Kilkenny in 1982 – see p. 95). But the factors mentioned on p. 96 were also responsible for the anomalous results.

STV, then, is not a totally proportional system, and it can lead to anomalous results such as would not occur in the West German system, where the 5 per cent threshold requirement is the only deviation from pure proportionality. Advocates of proportional representation for Britain could find themselves embarrassed if, after all the effort that would be required to introduce a proportional system, the first result turned out to be one which gave the most seats to a party which had not received the most votes.

The chances of such a result occurring are, admittedly, remote. Moreover, in a political system such as Britain's, in which there are three groupings competing for power, an anomalous result would not have such serious consequences as in a two-party system such as Malta's. For the party with the most seats will be unlikely to secure an overall majority, and so, even if the 'wrong' party wins, it will still be unable to form a Government without the aid of coalition partners.

Nevertheless, the possibility of such an anomalous result is one that must give electoral reformers pause. It constitutes a defect in the STV system which must be borne in mind together with the system's undeniable advantages.

How would STV Operate in Britain?

Let us consider what the result of the British general election of 1983 would have been if STV had been in operation in Britain. Obviously, we will have to make some drastically simplifying assumptions — for example (and both of these assumptions are perhaps unlikely), that voting habits would remain the same under a different electoral system and that the results would not be affected by the pattern of inter-party transfers.

Also, of course, the outcome would depend on how the constituencies were grouped together. A number of detailed proposals have been made for the division of Britain into multi-member constituencies. One of the most recent is that produced by the joint Liberal/SDP Alliance Commission on Constitutional Reform, published in July 1982. This Commission proposed that Britain be divided up in the following way:*

1-member constituencies	4
2-member constituencies	9
3-member constituencies	25
4-member constituencies	29
5-member constituencies	48
6-member constituencies	23
7-member constituencies	3
8-member constituencies	2
Total	143 constituencies (628 seats)

* It did not discuss Northern Ireland.

A calculation of the likely result of the 1983 general election using STV in constituencies drawn up as above has been made by Mr Brian Whitt. The result, according to Mr Whitt, would have been as follows:

Conservatives	269 seats
Labour	191 seats
Alliance	166 seats
Scottish National Party	5 seats
Plaid Cymru	2 seats

This result comes remarkably close to that which a totally proportional system would give (see p. 7). Mr Whitt, however, does not, perhaps, take full account of the fact that under STV a party which can attract later preferences can secure more seats than its total of first preferences would seem to warrant. For this reason, it may be that he under-estimates the number of seats which the Alliance would win.

STV would not only alter the number of MPs returned from each party; it would also alter the geographical distribution of MPs from each party. At present, as we have seen, the South of England (outside London) is dominated almost entirely by the Conservative, while the inner-city conurbations of the north are dominated by Labour. This would not be the case under STV.

In multi-member constituencies all three of the major political groupings would succeed in winning at least one seat in almost every part of the country. Oxfordshire, for example, which in 1983 returned six Conservative MPs for about 50 per cent of the vote, would under STV probably return three Conservative MPs, two Alliance MPs and one Labour MP. Liverpool, which returned six Labour MPs and one Alliance MP in 1983, would under STV probably return two Conservative, three Labour and two Alliance MPs.*

STV, unlike the British electoral system, would ensure that the main political groupings were represented in every part of

* Brian Whitt, *Election 83: An Alliance Perspective*, published privately (Cambridge, 1983), pp. 19–23.

the country. STV could achieve this outcome far more effectively than the German system which, because it retains the single-member constituency, would not avoid the geographical distortions characteristic of the British electoral system. STV, therefore, is the system most likely to ensure that the Conservative minority in Liverpool and the Labour minority in the south of England would secure representation in the Commons. This would be likely to have beneficial effects upon the workings of government, since it would make the Conservatives more sensitive to the problems of the inner cities and urban unemployment and Labour more aware of the problems of regions outside the depressed areas of the north and Scotland.

There would also be an incentive for candidates to stand for the Commons in the area in which they live and which they know best. At present those who live in Hampshire and wish to stand for the Commons as Labour candidates are wasting their time if they seek a seat in Hampshire. They must migrate to inner London or the north of England. Similarly, Conservatives in Liverpool must find a seat elsewhere if they seriously want to win. In the Irish Republic, by contrast, almost every member of the Dail has been a long standing resident of the constituency which he or she represents and is well known personally to his or her constituents.

Since STV comprises both a general election and a primary election, the element of personality is quite crucial. No member of the Dail can be assured of a safe seat, even if his or her party is strong in the constituency. There may be safe seats for particular parties, but there can be none for a particular candidate, who is always liable to be defeated by another candidate from the same party. In the election of November 1982, for example, nine of the 23 constituency changes – including Gibbons at Carlow–Kilkenny – involved members of the Dail who were defeated by other members of the same party.

The MP/Constituency Relationship

Because personal popularity is so important to candidates who stand for election under STV, they will do all they can to differentiate themselves from their competitors. One method of doing this is to adopt a distinctive policy stance. In Britain a Labour candidate might, for example, appear before the electorate as a unilateralist; a Conservative might choose to stand as a 'wet' in favour of reflating the economy. But in Ireland policy differences between candidates of the same party are not as common as attempts to win support through offering good constituency service.

If the same were to happen in Britain, STV would dramatically improve the quality of representation. The system would make it essential for an MP to be a good constituency Member if he wished to keep his seat. Under the British electoral system there is no similar incentive for an MP from a safe seat. He may be a very poor constituency representative, as well as being inadequate at his job in Westminster, but this would be unlikely to cost him more than 2,000 votes at the very outside. No doubt the majority of MPs are perfectly conscientious, but nevertheless the electoral system in Britain can serve to protect the lazy MP.

The single-member constituency, and the close relationship which this supposedly fosters between constituent and MP, has long been regarded as one of the strongest features of the British electoral system, something which any scheme of proportional representation would inevitably destroy, either by requiring a party list, as in Germany, or by requiring multi-member constituencies, as in Ireland. Indeed, the main objection made to STV is that it secures proportionality only by establishing mammoth multi-member constituencies. STV constituencies would, of course, be much larger in Britain than in the Irish Republic. In Ireland the average size of a five-member constituency is about 70,000, while in Britain – unless the number of seats in the Commons were enlarged – it would be about 325,000.

There has, however, been little examination of the realities of the much vaunted relationship between MPs and constituents. The principal study which attempts to evaluate this derives from a survey conducted by National Opinion Polls for Granada Television in 1972. This suggested that 47 per cent of the electorate were unaware of their MP's name; 49 per cent had not heard or read about their MP in the last year; 77 per cent were unable to mention anything done by their MP in Parliament; and 81 per cent were unable to mention anything done by their MP for their constituency.

TABLE 8   *Constituency contact with MP: comparison between London and the south-west*

	London (%)	South-west (%)	All (%)
Knew name of MP	41	79	53
Could recall something that MP had done in Parliament	21	37	23
Could recall something that MP had done for constituency	18	30	19

What is surprising is that relationships seemed to be better in large rural constituencies than in small urban ones. It appeared that there was a greater degree of familiarity and contact with the local MP in the south-west, where six out of seven constituencies surveyed were rural and some were far-flung, than in Greater London (see table 8).* These figures do not, of course, prove that contact between MPs and constituents would be better with multi-member constituencies. Indeed, London, it might be argued, is a very special case because of its highly mobile population and its constituency structure, which hardly corresponds with natural community

* Ivor Crewe, 'Electoral Reform and the Local MP', in S. E. Finer (ed.), *Adversary Politics and Electoral Reform* (London, Wigram, 1975), p. 333.

boundaries. Moreover, under STV constituencies would be far larger than even the most far-flung constituencies anywhere in Britain today. Under the Alliance proposals, for example, the county of Somerset would become one single five-member constituency rather than five large rural constituencies.

Nevertheless, the figures given in table 8 do suggest that constituency size is not the *only*, and perhaps not even the *main*, determinant of the quality of the relationship between constituents and MPs. It is plausible to argue that this relationship could be sustained, and possibly even improved, with multi-member constituencies in which there was competition both between parties and between candidates to provide a good service for constituents.

The results of the Granada survey do not bear out the self-congratulatory picture of the relationship between constituents and MPs so often painted by defenders of the British electoral system. It may even be that the single-member constituency actually deters some constituents from contacting their MP. Private landlords living in Oldham West, for example, might not feel entirely at ease contacting their MP, Michael Meacher; while radical students living in Finchley might feel that Margaret Thatcher, their constituency MP, would not be wholly sympathetic to their point of view. Moreover, because of the convention that one MP does not encroach upon the constituency of another, a constituent has no redress if he finds his MP unsatisfactory.

With STV, on the other hand, such problems would hardly arise. In each constituency there would be MPs from each of the main parties and probably a balanced slate of MPs reflecting the different social elements in the constituency. In the Irish Republic multi-member constituencies are not thought to make for a poor relationship between members and constituents. On the contrary, the complaint is often heard that the relationship is too close – that members of the Dail have become little more than glorified constituency welfare officers. They have to spend so much time looking after their constituents that they are unable to devote attention to the issues of policy which come before the Dail. Consequently, the Government finds itself relatively free from scrutiny in the Dail and can carry through its policies without worrying about opposition from Parliament.

Such a pattern persists, of course, only because it is the wish of the voters. They could, if they so wished, support candidates who would concentrate more upon the scrutiny of legislation than upon constituency service. STV allows – indeed, encourages – constituents to vote for the kind of representative they want. It is, in this sense, a *transparent* electoral system, one in which the elected representatives tend to reflect the qualities of those who elect them. STV is an electoral system which holds up a mirror to society.

Would STV Result in Political Stability?

STV is usually defended as a method of securing proportional representation but attacked on the ground that multi-member constituencies, which the system necessarily requires, make for less effective constituency representation. Paradoxically, however, as we have found, STV is not quite as proportional as is often assumed and can, indeed, produce perverse results, but it is likely to yield a far better quality of representation than can be obtained by other electoral systems. STV is a little less fair than is commonly supposed but probably makes for more effective representation.

In Ireland there is a high degree of satisfaction with the system. Twice – in referendums in 1959 and 1968 – voters have resisted proposals by the Government of the day (Fianna Fail in each case) to change the system. Turnout is generally at around the same level as in Britain; this means that it is in reality much higher, since there is no postal voting in Ireland, and a large proportion of the population works outside the country.

Proportional representation is often attacked on the grounds that it encourages political instability and extremism. Yet in Ireland it seems to have had the opposite effect. The

Irish state was born in 1922 in conditions of violence and civil war; the Opposition, led by De Valera, refused to take its seats in the Dail until 1927, five years after the state was founded and after it had been defeated in a murderous civil war. 'This is not,' one member of the Dail declared in 1958, when the Government was seeking to abolish proportional representation, 'the United States of America. This is not Great Britain. Harold Macmillan has not fought Hugh Gaitskell in a civil war. Nobody looks across the floor of an English Parliament to recall that his father may have fallen at the hands of another member's father. . . .'* Yet STV has accompanied, and has perhaps helped to assist in, the gradual healing of wounds. Since the mid-1930s the Irish Republic has remained almost entirely free of threats from anti- parliamentary groups, and its political system is highly stable.

This generalization is only apparently undermined by the fact that there were three general elections in the Irish Republic within the space of eighteen months in 1981 and 1982, for this was the first time there had been a deadlock in Ireland for forty years. The difficulties of 1981 and 1982 are best seen as the kind of interregnum which can occur even in stable countries under any electoral system, and did in fact occur in Britain between 1922 and 1924 when there were three general elections within two years. Indeed, if there is a criticism to be made of Irish politics, it would be that it is *too* stable rather than unstable, since the differences between the two major parties are too narrow to sustain a sufficiently vigorous debate on the future of the country.

In 1922 the acting chairman of the committee whose task it was to draw up a constitution for the new Irish state declared, 'It is certain that in Ireland many parties will be present in the chamber. It will be impossible according to the English method to form a Government without coalition in which

* Quoted in Cornelius O'Leary, *Irish Elections, 1918–1977: Parties, Voters and Proportional Representation* (Dublin, Gill & Macmillan, 1979), p. 51.

there will be inevitable "jockeying" for ministerial power.'* Yet neither of these predictions – that there would be a large number of parties in the Dail, and that coalition government would be the norm – have been realized.

Far from the electoral system having encouraged a proliferation of small parties, the number of parties represented in the Dail steadily decreased between 1922 and 1981. In 1923 there were no fewer than nineteen competing groups standing for election, and over one-fifth of the seats in the Dail were won by candidates not belonging to the three major parties, Fianna Fail, Fine Gael and Labour. Between 1969 and 1981, however, these three parties were the only ones to achieve representation in the Dail: and in the election of November 1982, although a fourth party, the Workers Party did succeed in winning two seats, the three major parties secured between them nearly 94 per cent of the vote and all but four of the 166 seats in the Dail.

This gradual decline in the number of parties must be partly due to the fact that multi-member constituencies allow a much wider range of political opinion to be expressed by candidates from the same party than is possible in a single-member constituency system such as the British. With STV there might have never have been a Social Democrat breakaway from the Labour Party, since right-wing Labour candidates could have stood in tandem with the left and asked the voters to choose between them. Further, under STV the parties would be chary of exerting strong discipline over their MPs because a breakaway candidate would have a far greater chance of holding his seat than under Britain's present electoral system. It is easier to secure 17 per cent of the vote in a five-member constituency than, say, 40 per cent of the vote in a single-member constituency. Many of the SDP MPs who lost their seats in the British general election in 1983 might well have succeeded in holding them in the multi-member constituencies under STV.

* Quoted in Brian Farrell, 'Coalitions and Political Institutions: the Irish Experience', in Vernon Bogdanor (ed.), *Coalition Government in Western Europe* (London, Heinemann, 1983), p. 249.

Indeed, it is precisely because it allows for the expression of intra-party dissent that the single transferable vote is so distrusted by party leaders and officials. It can fairly be claimed that this system tends to weaken parties, thereby making them less coherent organizations for the promotion of social change. In places where highly disciplined parties are backed up by powerful party machines, the STV emphasizes the personal qualities of the candidate, and in the Irish Republic candidates have developed sophisticated personal machines to ensure that votes are cast for them and not for their rivals. It is this very feature of the system – the competition between candidates of the same party – which leads most politicians to dislike it but prompts many voters to support it.

The second prediction – that government in Ireland would consist predominantly of coalitions marked by continual jockeying for power – has also been falsified by Ireland's experience, for, since the founding of the state in 1922 single-party government has been the norm. Indeed, twice in the last 50 years Fianna Fail has governed for an unbroken period of 16 years, from 1932 to 1948, and from 1957 to 1973; while the average length of life of Governments since the war, three years and three months, is exactly the same as in Britain.

There have been only five coalitions since the state was founded, spanning (by 1984) a total of 13 years. Coalitions, however, have operated very much like single-party Governments, and have, on the whole, maintained the conventions associated with single-party government such as collective Cabinet responsibility and a unified approach to policy issues. Indeed, what is perhaps surprising is that although Ireland's electoral system is so different from that used in Britain, its governmental arrangements adhere extraordinarily closely to those of the Westminster model.

Perhaps the greatest difficulty facing advocates of STV in Britain is that the system has been used only in small rural societies. The experience of countries such as Ireland and Malta is not necessarily a good guide to how STV might work in Britain, for it is difficult to distinguish between the consequences of the electoral system itself and those which flow from a society where political divisions are as much 'tribal' as they are socio-economic in nature. STV has never been tried in a predominantly urban industrial society, and no sure predictions can be made of the consequences of adopting it in such a society. To adopt STV in Britain, therefore, would be a risk; but it is a risk which many would be prepared to take in order to secure its undoubted benefits.

6

Women and Ethnic Minorities

The Representation of Women

The title of this chapter may appear surprising. There does not, at first sight, seem to be any connection between a country's electoral system and the number of women or members of ethnic minorities able to gain election to its Parliament. It is the purpose of this chapter, however, to show that there *is* a close relationship between the two. There can be little doubt that either the German system or STV would increase the number of women and ethnic minorities who would gain election to the House of Commons. Indeed, the existence of such a relationship can be stated with a far higher degree of confidence than is usually possible in matters of political debate, for 'It is the unanimous finding of all those studies which have been explicitly concerned with the linkage between women's legislative representation and the nature of the electoral system that systems of proportional representation appear to favour higher levels of female representation.'*

In every parliament in the world women and ethnic minorities find themselves considerably under-represented in relation to their numbers in the population. The reasons for this are no doubt highly complex, having to do with cultural factors and social conditioning as well as overt prejudice. These factors themselves are, of course, quite independent of

* Francis G. Castles, 'Female Legislative Representation and the Electoral System', *Politics*, vol. 1, no. 2 (November 1981), p. 22.

the method of election, but their effects can be minimized or exaggerated by the electoral system which a society adopts.

Britain offers a particularly flagrant example of the under-representation of women and ethnic minorities. There has been no black or Asian MP in Britain since the 1920s: the only minority representatives in Parliament are, paradoxically in the House of Lords, where there is a West Indian peer, Lord Pitt, and an Asian, Lord Chitnis.

There have been women MPs in the Commons since 1918, when the first woman MP was elected, but women have always formed a minuscule proportion of the House (see table 9). Although women constitute over half the population in Britain, they have never comprised even 5 per cent of the House of Commons. It is hardly surprising that movements which seek the advancement of women are searching eagerly for methods of remedying this state of affairs; there is currently in Britain an organization known as the 300 Group, whose aim it is to raise the level of women's representation until there are 300 women in the Commons, for only if women

TABLE 9   *Women in the House of Commons, 1945–83*

General election	No of women MPs returned	% of total number of MPs
1945	24	3.75
1950	21	3.36
1951	17	2.72
1955	24	3.81
1959	25	3.97
1964	29	4.60
1966	26	4.13
1970	26	4.13
1974 (Feb.)	23	3.62
1974 (Oct.)	27	4.25
1979	19	2.99
1983	23	3.54

are more strongly represented in the Commons, so it believes, will legislation and government policy be able to take full account of the problems and specific viewpoint of the female majority of the electorate.

Why are women so dramatically under-represented in Britain? Even if we take into account the complex social and cultural factors involved, there can be no doubt that selection committees are hesitant to choose women candidates. This does not necessarily mean that the selection committees themselves are prejudiced. They may well be, of course, but it is equally likely that they may believe that the *electorate* is prejudiced. They may believe that, other things being equal, a woman candidate could lose vital votes for their party; and they will feel it their duty – understandably – to choose the candidate who can best maximize their party's support. The fact that there is no evidence whatever for the belief that a woman candidate is likely to deter male voters* will not necessarily prevent selection committees from erring on the side of caution. They will tend to choose a 'safe' candidate who will be as near to an identikit model of an MP as it is possible to find. The candidate will be white, middle-aged – and male.

If we now look at table 10, showing the percentage of women represented in different legislatures, we can see that in countries such as Canada, New Zealand and the USA which, like Britain, have a single-member constituency system, the level of women's representation is also low. It tends to be marginally higher in countries using STV but can be very considerably higher in countries which, like West Germany, use party list systems of proportional representation.

Some of the results in table 10 are quite surprising. It can be seen that the USA, which has a thriving women's movement, has a smaller percentage of women in its national legislature than countries where attitudes to women are far more traditional, such as Ireland, Portugal, Italy and Switzerland, which did not even give women the vote in federal elections

* See Elizabeth Vallance, 'Women Candidates and Elector Preference', *Politics*, vol. 1, no. 2 (November 1981).

TABLE 10   *The representation of women in different legislatures*

Type of electoral system	Women representatives as % of total
Single-member constituencies	
Britain (1983)	3.5
USA (1978)	3.7
New Zealand (1980)	4.3
Canada (1980)	5.0
Single transferable vote	
Malta (1981)	4.6
Ireland (November 1982)	8.4
Party list systems	
Israel (1981)	6.6
Belgium (1978)	7.5
Portugal (1981)	7.5
Italy (1977)	8.4
Germany (1983)	9.8
Austria (1981)	10.0
Switzerland (1981)	10.5
Netherlands (1977)	15.3
Norway (1977)	22.5
Sweden (1981)	22.6
Denmark (1979)	23.4
Finland (1979)	26.0

until 1971. It is noticeable that *all* of the countries with party lists have a larger percentage of women in their legislatures than any country using the British single-member constituency system. In the four Scandinavian countries around one-quarter of the legislature are women.

This difference between the participation of women in public life in Scandinavia and Britain does not seem to be due, as might at first be thought, to a more generally enlightened attitude towards women's participation in Scandinavia. For the proportion of women doctors in Finland and Norway is far lower than in Britain – 8 per cent and 12 per cent respectively –as compared with a figure of 22 per cent in Britain; and the figures for the percentage of women university professors is also low in the Scandinavian countries.

There must, it seems, be another reason for the discrepancy. In what way might the representation of women be affected by the electoral system? It seems plausible to suppose that whereas a selection committee may hesitate to choose a woman as a candidate in a single-member constituency, a committee choosing a party list will be concerned to secure a 'balanced ticket'. Since the list contains a large number of names, it is unlikely that any voter will be deterred from supporting a party by the presence of women. But the absence of women in high places on the list will cause offence and will narrow the appeal of the party. A party will not wish to advertise its prejudice by placing women low down on the list. For whereas under a single-member constituency system it is the *presence* of a candidate who deviates from the identikit norm (whether female or black) that is noticed, in a party list system it is the *absence* of a woman or minority candidate, the *failure* to present a balanced ticket, that will be commented upon and resented.

Moreover, a party list system offers a focus for women to organize to achieve higher levels of representation. In the Netherlands a women's group persuaded the Dutch Labour Party to ensure that 25 per cent of its candidates are women, while in the Swedish Liberal and Social Democratic parties, there are pressures for alternate representation of male and female candidates on the party list or, alternatively, for at least 40 per cent of the candidates to be women.

There is, fortunately, a simple way of testing the argument that a list system is more likely than a single-member constituency system to encourage women's representation: by comparing, over a period of time, the percentage of women who have achieved election to the German Bundestag. Since the German electoral system, as we have seen, comprises two elements — a single-member constituency element, as in Britain, and a party list element — we can easily compare the number of women elected by the two methods (see table 11). It is quite clear that women fare much better under the party list than in the single-member constituencies. Given the conclusiveness of such figures, there can hardly be room for doubt that the introduction into Britain of an electoral system of the German type could significantly improve the representation of women in the Commons.

TABLE 11   *Women representatives elected to the Bundestag, 1949–83*

Year	No. of women elected from constituencies	No. of women elected from the party lists
1949	12	15
1953	9	31
1957	9	35
1961	7	33
1965	8	25
1969	5	27
1972	4	24
1976	7	29
1980	11	30
1983	10	39

The same result would not, however, be achieved by the Hansard Society's variant of the German system. For this relies totally upon the single-member constituency, and the 'list' is in reality a hidden one, comprising the best losers from those parties which the single-member constituency system under-represents. Every candidate must stand in a single-member constituency, as in the British electoral system. From the point of view of women's representation, therefore, the Hansard

Society's system would offer no improvement on Britain's present electoral system.

STV, however, as table 10 shows, does promise some advantage to female candidates as compared with the British-type electoral system but not as great an advantage as party list systems, even though the table probably under-states the improvement in terms of women's representation which might be obtained by the adoption of STV in Britain, since cultural attitudes to women in Britain are rather more advanced than in such traditional societies as Ireland and Malta.

With multi-member constituencies, as required by STV, there will be pressure upon constituency selection committees to present a balanced list of candidates. By contrast with the single-member constituency system, the absence of a female from a party's slate of candidates in the constituency is likely to be noticed. People who are prejudiced against women can hardly object if there are one, two or even three women candidates representing their party in a five-member constit-uency, for they can, if they so choose, make a male candidate their first preference. But if there is a 'women's vote', the party concerned will forfeit support unless it presents women candidates. In Ireland in the November 1982 general election nearly half – 19 out of 41 – of the constituencies had at least one woman candidate from one of the major parties. Where there is a genuine 'woman's vote' it can, through the process of inter-party transfers secure the election of women members to the Dail. There is, indeed, some evidence that women in Ireland are beginning to use their voting power in this way for the explicit purpose of electing women candidates. STV would make possible in Britain a large increase in the number of women MPs if that was the wish of the electorate.

The Representation of Ethnic Minorities

Ethnic minorities are even more unfortunate than women from the point of view of parliamentary representation.

Britain's black and Asian population, at around 2¼ million, forms about 4 per cent of the population and is highly concentrated in particular conurbations, there being 19 constituencies where the proportion of the population with New Commonwealth or Pakistan roots is over 25 per cent. Yet the ethnic minorities have been unable to elect MPs of their own. This is not only harmful to the minority communities but also a loss to Parliament itself and to the white population which is unable to apprehend the point of view of sections of Britain's population that are deeply affected by much of the legislation produced at Westminster.

The Commons continually debates the condition of the ethnic minority population without such debates being informed by the presence of any member of this minority. How can such debates hope to reach satisfactory conclusions? The Parliament of 1979–83 was forced to consider the causes of the inner-city riots which broke out in a number of British cities in 1981 and took MPs – even those living in the areas concerned – entirely by surprise. Yet the absence of minority representatives from the debates meant that their interests were likely to be excluded, and it made a hollow mockery of the claim of the House of Commons to be a mirror of the nation.

As with women candidates, party selection committees are highly unlikely to offer winnable seats to candidates from ethnic minorities. Even if they are not prejudiced themselves, they may believe that a black or Asian candidate is likely to lose their party support, and as good party members they will feel it their duty to do all that they can to maximize votes for their party.

By contrast with the case of women candidates, there seems some reason to believe that the electorate does in fact display prejudice towards black or Asian candidates. In 1970 Dr David (now Lord) Pitt was selected as a Labour candidate to fight Clapham. He lost the Labour-held seat on a swing of over 10 per cent against him, although the swing to the Conservatives in the neighbouring constituencies was considerably less. In the general election of 1983 there were only 17 black or Asian candidates out of the 2,575 fighting the election. In the eight constituencies fought by Alliance candidates who were Asians or black, the Alliance vote rose on average by only 6 per cent as compared with 13 per cent in equivalent constituencies where the Alliance candidates were white; while some, but not all, black and Asian Labour and Conservative candidates also performed less well than white candidates in equivalent constituencies.

Reasoning similar to that used in the discussion of women's representation makes it appear likely that either the German electoral system or STV would be more likely to lead to the election of black or Asian MPs than the British system. With a party list system the absence of minority candidates in high positions on a party list would be noticed, and if the return of black or Asian MPs was a priority to a particular community, this would deter minority voters from voting for the party concerned. Since black or Asian candidates would remain a minority on the party list, their presence would not have a similar deterrent effect on the racially prejudiced. Indeed, their election would help to overcome prejudice, since it would raise the esteem – and the self-esteem – of the various minority communities.

STV would offer the ethnic minorities an excellent opportunity to elect MPs who were truly representative of their communities and, if they so wished, to vote for candidates across party lines so as to secure this outcome. In areas such as Birmingham or parts of London where there is a sizeable ethnic minority population the major parties would find it prudent to present at least one ethnic minority candidate – and probably more – in each multi-member constituency. Indeed, this phenomenon can already be seen in local government elections, many of which, although retaining the British first-past-the-post electoral system, are held in multi-member wards. It was this that enabled Dr David Pitt to secure election as one of the Labour Party's candidates for the London County Council in 1961 in Stoke Newington and Hackney

North. Pitt was eventually to become chairman of the Greater London Council, the LCC's successor, and a member of the House of Lords which, from the point of view of providing a forum for minorities, has proved more representative than the Commons!

In a five-member constituency the quota needed to secure election under STV is, as we have seen, 17 per cent. According to the 1981 census, in 22 of the 32 London boroughs over 10 per cent of the population live in a household whose head was born in the New Commonwealth. Therefore the minority population would be able to form a powerful voting bloc, able to elect candidates who could further its interests. Under the proposals produced by the Liberal/SDP Alliance Commission for the division of Britain into multi-member constituencies (see p. 100) six London constituencies would be likely to elect a black or Asian MP, for in these six constituencies the proportion of the population living in a household whose head was born in the New Commonwealth would be at least equal to the quota.

There is evidence also from the USA that STV would assist minority candidates. For this system was used to elect the city council in Cincinatti, Ohio, between 1925 and 1957, and during this period one or two blacks were regularly elected to the council on as little as 10 per cent of the vote, while after the abolition of STV in 1957 this was no longer so. The same pattern was noticeable in New York, where the city council was elected by STV between 1937 and 1945, the abolition of STV being strongly opposed by the National Association for the Advancement of Colored Peoples.*

There can, then, be little doubt that either the German system or STV would encourage the election of black and Asian candidates to the Commons, perhaps in quite significant

* John Curtice, 'Proportional Representation and Britain's Ethnic Minorities: Various Electoral Systems and their Implications for the Black and Jewish Communities', *Contemporary Affairs Briefing* (London, Centre for Contemporary Affairs), vol. 2, no. 6 (February 1983). This pamphlet contains an admirable exposition of the issues involved.

numbers, and this would improve the quality not only of representation but also of political justice in Britain. For, as John Morley declared almost a hundred years ago, 'The best guarantee of justice in public dealings is the participation in their own government of the people most likely to suffer from injustice.'*

Proportional Representation and the National Front

These advantages which proportional representation would yield for ethnic minorities would be more than counter-balanced, in the eyes of many, if it were also to assist the chances of election of candidates representing anti-immigrant parties such as the National Front. No candidate from the National Front or any similar organization has ever been able to win election to the House of Commons. But critics of proportional representation often suggest that it helps small, extremist parties. Would this work to the advantage of parties such as the National Front, enabling them to achieve what they cannot at present hope to attain – representation in the Commons?

Our analysis of the workings of two very different proportional representation systems in Germany and Ireland suggest that fears of this kind are probably misplaced. In Germany neo-Nazi candidates have been unable to win election to the Bundestag, although in 1969 they came close to surmounting the 5 per cent threshold needed to secure representation. In Ireland extremist candidates have on occasion been elected to the Dail. In 1957 Sinn Fein, then the political wing of the IRA, won four seats, only to lose them again in 1961, while in 1981 two H-block prisoners in Northern Ireland gained election to the Dail. It should, however be remembered that an H-block prisoner and a member of Sinn Fein were also returned to Westminster in by-elections in Fermanagh and South Tyrone in 1981, while in the general election of 1983 Gerry Adams,

* John Morley, *On Compromise* (London, Macmillan, 1886), p. 326.

the vice-president of Sinn Fein, was elected to the Commons as MP for West Belfast. It seems to be the Irish question itself, rather than the use of any particular electoral system, which leads to the return of candidates from extreme parties. Further, it is worth reiterating that under STV the Republic of Ireland has developed from civil war to stable democracy. There is no evidence that it has encouraged extremism, and it has probably played a conciliatory role in healing old wounds.

However, when the suggestion is made that proportional representation encourages extremism, it is not the post-war experience of countries such as Germany and Ireland which critics have in mind but the collapse of democracy in Central Europe between the wars and, in particular, the destruction of weak parliamentary regimes in Germany and Italy by Hitler and Mussolini. In Italy proportional representation was introduced in 1919, and two elections were held under it before Mussolini's accession to power in 1922. In Germany proportional representation was also introduced in 1919 with the Weimar Republic, Germany's first experiment with democracy. Racked from the beginning by extremism from right and left, the Republic did not settle down to any sort of stability until 1924. This stability, however, lasted only five years, and it was destroyed by the slump of 1929. In 1930 the Nazis became the second largest party in Germany and in 1932 the largest, although it was not until 1933 that Hitler became Chancellor of Germany.

The background to the problems faced by Italy and Germany in the 1920s was very different from that faced by democratic governments today. In Italy parliamentary government had never gained esteem, and after the First World War the large Socialist Party was only partially committed to parliamentary government, many of its members preferring industrial sit-ins and occupations. This, together with the fear of communism after the Russian Revolution, led to a demand for 'strong government' from the right, something which Mussolini was very willing to supply.

In Germany the Weimar Republic was handicapped from

the start by being associated with the country's military defeat and humiliation in the First World War. Many of Germany's military and administrative elite were hostile to the democratic experiment and hankered for the return of a monarchical or authoritarian regime. These elements were strengthened by the great inflation of 1923, which wiped out the savings of the middle class and made it excessively fearful of any Government of the left which, it believed, would inflate the currency. It was natural, therefore, for many among the German electorate to blame the fledgling Republic for the depression and to believe that Hitler was a saviour who alone could bring about recovery.

The political atmosphere in Britain in the last part of the twentieth century is, fortunately, quite different from that of Germany and Italy in the 1920s. Britain has a long-established tradition of parliamentary government, and there are no significant groups in society seeking to overthrow it. The electorate has firmly refused to support any extremist grouping whose allegiance to democracy is in any way in doubt. It would take a political earthquake to alter such deep-rooted beliefs.

Nor is it at all plausible to blame the electoral system for Mussolini and Hitler. It is difficult to believe that a movement of the force and sweep of Hitler's Nazis could have been stopped by any alternative electoral system. Indeed, under the British electoral system the Nazis, as the second largest party in 1930, would have become the official Opposition, while in 1932 they would have formed a Government with an absolute majority in Parliament some months before Hitler became Chancellor of a coalition in which the Nazis were in a minority. At Nuremberg Hermann Göring insisted that under the British electoral system the Nazis would have won every single seat in Germany in 1932, and this was by no means an implausible assertion, given the devastated state of the country. For the British electoral system, it must be remembered, over-represents large parties at the expense of smaller ones, and after 1930 the Nazis were definitely a major party of the state, winning the votes of almost every German who was opposed to socialism and communism.

In European countries with more stable political backgrounds and more deep-rooted democratic traditions, proportional representation proved, in the inter-war years, perfectly compatible with a moderate style of government. Scandinavia between the wars was remarkable not for the growth of extremist politics but for the dominance of the Social Democrats, who pioneered new methods of social welfare and economic management; while Czechoslavakia, which had almost the same electoral system as the Weimar Republic in Germany, managed to sustain a stable democracy until subverted by Nazi Germany in the late 1930s.

The proportional systems most likely to be adopted in Britain, the German electoral system or STV, both have provisions designed to exclude very small parties. In Germany no party failing to obtain 5 per cent of the total vote will secure representation, while in Ireland the size of the constituency quota acts as a threshold which small parties have to surmount. By contrast, the German electoral system in the 1920s and the Italian system before Mussolini lacked such thresholds. They were therefore susceptible to the intrusion of minor extremist parties, unable or unwilling to participate in government but in a position to undermine the authority of Parliament.

The electoral support which the National Front has received, even in its years of comparative success in the 1970s, fall short of what it would need to win a seat under either the German system or STV. In the 1983 general election the National Front polled an average of only 1.0 per cent per candidate, and its highest percentage vote in any constituency was 3.7 per cent in Newham South. Its best performance in a general election was in 1970, when 10 candidates secured an average of 3.6 per cent of the vote. In February 1974, 54 candidates gained an average of 3.3 per cent of the vote, while in October 1974, 90 candidates gained an average of 3.1 per cent of the vote. The National Front, therefore, would not succeed in surmounting the STV quota in a multi-member constituency, nor would it be likely to surmount the lower threshold of the German system, 5 per cent in the country as a whole, nor even 5 per cent in any region.

However, in 1977 the National Front *did* succeed in just surmounting the 5 per cent threshold in the Greater London Council elections, and so it is possible that if there had been a 5 per cent regional threshold, the National Front *would* have gained a London seat in the Commons under the German electoral system in 1977. It is fair to say, however, that voters may be less willing to support a small party in an election for a Government than in an election for a local authority, where a protest vote can be indulged with impunity.

The National Front would have a better opportunity of winning a seat if, as a result of the introduction of proportional representation, voting habits were to change, for the fear that supporting a small party might mean wasting one's vote would be much diminished under either the German system or STV. The German system offers an incentive to vote for a small party, provided only that it can achieve 5 per cent of the vote; while under STV if a vote is cast for a candidate who cannot win, it is not wasted but instead transferred to another candidate. So a voter intending to support the National Front need have no anxiety that he will be splitting the vote and letting the candidate he least favours win the seat.

It is, of course, impossible to predict how voting habits might change under a system of proportional representation, but there seems no reason to believe that a party which preaches hostility to immigrants would be able to increase its support. In the 1983 general election immigration was, for most voters, a less important political issue than at any general election since the mid-1950s. It may be that, with the ending of large-scale immigration into Britain, the issue is no longer one capable of stirring electoral passions, but, of course, one cannot be sure.

There must remain, therefore, the very slight possibility that proportional representation would encourage the election of one or two extremist candidates to the House of Commons.

Such a result would be more likely with the German electoral system than with STV, since the former imposes a lower threshold upon small parties. This possibility, the election of a National Front MP, however remote, must be balanced against the advantages which systems of proportional representation are likely to yield to candidates representing the ethnic minorities. It seems hardly possible to doubt that, on balance, proportional representation would offer very considerable benefits to members of minority communities, which would be likely to strengthen their position in British society.

7

Some Consequences of Proportional Representation

What would be the main consequences of introducing one of the two types of proportional representation which we have discussed into Britain? How would proportional representation alter the workings of the British constitution? What would the implications be for institutions such as the Cabinet and the House of Commons? How would the party system be affected? The answers to such questions depend not only upon the specific qualities of the electoral systems themselves but also upon the traditions and political culture of a country, for similar electoral systems can have widely different effects in different countries, as we saw in chapter 6.

Despite the difficulties involved in making speculative judgements, some account must be given of the likely implications of proportional representation if a balanced verdict is to be reached. For if proportional representation were to involve a complex and far-reaching constitutional upheaval, then many who might otherwise be prepared to support it could be excused for having second thoughts. This chapter, therefore, is a short essay in conjecture, an attempt to chart the kinds of change which would follow the introduction of a new electoral system.

Many of the consequences of proportional representation flow from the fact that, under a proportional system, general elections would be unlikely to yield an overall majority in the

Commons for any one party. The task of governing the country, therefore, would have to be undertaken either by a single-party minority Government or, alternatively, by a coalition of two (or more) parties.

This would be a comparatively novel experience for Britain, for only three general elections since 1918 – the elections of 1923, 1929 and February 1974 – have failed to produce an overall majority for one party. On each occasion the result was a short-lived minority Labour Government. Britain was also governed by a minority Labour administration between April 1976, when the Labour Government elected by a small overall majority in October 1974 found that its majority had disappeared as a result of a by-election loss and a defection, and May 1979, when it was defeated in the general election.

Coalition Governments in Britain, on the other hand, have been less a product of parliamentary arithmetic than of war or economic crisis. In May 1915, ten months after the outbreak of the First World War, the Prime Minister, H. H. Asquith, formed a coalition Government with the Conservatives and Labour. Asquith was overthrown in December 1916, but his successor, Lloyd George, also governed as head of a coalition which lasted until 1922, having gained massive endorsement from the electorate in the 'khaki election' of December 1918 held shortly after the end of the war. In the Second World War also single-party government did not prove adequate to the massive problems which the country faced. In May 1940, nine months after Britain declared war, Winston Churchill became Prime Minister and proceeded to form an all-party coalition which lasted until the end of the war in 1945.

The only other coalition which Britain has experienced since 1918 has been the National Government, formed in August 1931 to meet an economic crisis. This Government, which comprised Conservatives, Liberals and a small section of the Labour Party, had the character of an emergency administration, and, although it continued to rule throughout the 1930s, it had lost much of its coalition character by September 1932, when the Liberals resigned from the Government. The bulk of the Labour Party opposed the National Government from the start, and its hostility to that Government's economic policies gave Labour a distrust of peacetime coalitions which still persists.

These various episodes have, however, only limited value for predicting how coalitions and minority Governments might work under proportional representation. For such Governments have been seen as brief interregnums between single-party majority Governments which have always been considered the norm. It is for this reason that the various intervals of minority government or coalition have not led to any major constitutional innovations. Every such Government has been thought of as exceptional, and politicians expected that a return to single-party government would soon follow.

It is this expectation which the introduction of proportional representation would shatter.

The Alliance under a Proportional System

Assuming that voting habits did not change radically, an election held under proportional representation would not produce a single-party majority Government. Instead it would register the relative strength of the various parties as measured by popular votes. A Government would have to be constructed *after* all of the votes had been counted. Critics of proportional representation make much of this point and assert that it takes away from the voters the power which elections ought to give them, the power to choose a Government.

But, as we have seen, in Germany and in Ireland, parties generally indicate *before* the election which coalition partners they favour. So, although the German general election of 1983, did not for example, yield an overall majority for any party, there was no doubt about who should form a Government. For the Free Democrats had made it absolutely clear before the election that they favoured the Christian Democrats as coalition partners and would co-operate with them in government. Similarly, after the November 1982 election in

Ireland, although no party enjoyed an overall majority in the Dail, there was hardly any doubt that the Fianna Fail Prime Minister, Charles Haughey, would be defeated and a Fine Gael/Labour coalition installed under Garret FitzGerald, the Fine Gael leader.

In Britain the Liberal/SDP Alliance would clearly become a pivotal grouping after proportional representation. It would be sought as a partner by both Labour and the Conservatives, who would be highly unlikely to team up with each other to keep out the Alliance. The Alliance would thus benefit in two ways from the introduction of proportional representation. It would cease to be under-represented in the Commons in relation to its vote in the country; and, since a single-party majority Government would be unlikely, the Alliance would also benefit as a near-permanent coalition partner, as with the German Free Democrats.

Would the Alliance declare before an election as the German Free Democrats have done, who their coalition partners would be? The Alliance did not do so in 1983, nor did the Liberals in 1979 or 1974, when coalition might well have been the outcome of the general election. There were good tactical reasons for this. The Liberals wished to alienate neither their leftward-leaning supporters by declaring that they would ally with the Conservatives nor their rightward-leaning supporters by declaring that they would ally with Labour. They therefore refused to follow the example of the German Free Democrats by indicating a preference for a particular coalition partner.

It might not be possible for the Alliance to maintain such a position after the introduction of proportional representation, for it would be known in advance that the Alliance would enjoy considerable influence in deciding who should form the Government after the election – which was not the case in 1974, 1979 or 1983. The Alliance, therefore, would be under considerable pressure to indicate its preference. Were the Alliance to accede to this pressure, then a three-party grouping would have become, in effect, one offering the voter a choice of only two alternatives. If, for example, the Alliance decided before an election that it would ally with the Conservatives, the voter's choice would be between an Alliance/Conservative coalition and a single-party Labour Government, which would require (nearly) 50 per cent of the vote to be able to rule.

If the Alliance proved unwilling to make such a declaration, then negotiations would have to begin once the election outcome was known. But even in this situation it would be a mistake to think that the Alliance would enjoy a free hand, for it would be bound both by the wishes of its supporters and by the programme on which it had fought the election. It would have to be able to secure a real advance towards the realization of its programme if a coalition agreement with one of the other parties were to be at all credible. Its position, although a powerful one, would not necessarily be enviable.

The Choice of Government under Proportional Representation

When an election did not give rise to an overall majority for one party, and the pivot party – the Alliance – had not given a definite undertaking which party it would support in government, there would be bound to be some uncertainty as to who should be called to the Palace to form a Government when the incumbent Prime Minister resigned. The days immediately following the election would probably be taken up with inter-party negotiations. These negotiations would cover not only the political colour of the Government but also its programme and the designation of the Prime Minister. When the incumbent Prime Minister resigned, the Queen would have to decide whom to summon to the Palace for the purpose of forming a Government. This could involve her, unwittingly, in party politics, for the candidate first called to the Palace would enjoy a considerable advantage over all rivals, since he or she would have both the political initiative and the authority to offer posts in a Government and would also acquire the aura of power which could well permit the formation of a Government even if he or she did not at first appear a likely choice as Prime Minister.

In a politically tense situation of this kind the sovereign could easily be accused, in the heat of the party battle, of favouring one side rather than another. A multi-party contest of the kind which proportional representation would produce could easily lead to a situation in which any choice of Prime Minister by the sovereign would appear controversial. It would be vital for politicians to do all that they could to prevent such a situation from arising.

In Continental monarchies with proportional representation and multi-party systems, elaborate conventions have been developed to protect the monarch from political involvement. Sometimes the monarch appoints a mediator who sounds out opinion and searches for an agreed solution, which he can then present to the monarch. In Sweden the king's functions have been entirely devolved to the Speaker, so that the monarch retains only ceremonial functions, a solution which Tony Benn has recommended for Britain. Otherwise, in his view, a three-party system would replace first-past-the-post by 'first-past-the-Palace'.*

Proposals of this kind, however, are hardly likely to be suitable in Britain, for it would be extremely difficult to discover a mediator whom all parties would accept and trust as a genuine neutral; and, given the traditions of British constitutional monarchy, the sovereign would be loath to surrender his or her prerogative, since this could, in exceptional circumstances, be used to protect the constitution against abuse. For the same reason, Mr Benn's solution of devolving the monarch's function to the Speaker is hardly applicable in the British context. It would entirely alter the Speaker's position; for, instead of remaining above and, in a sense, apart from the political battle, he would become deeply involved in party negotiations and bargains, and this would detract from his authority in the Commons.

There is only one way in which the sovereign can be protected from political embarrassment in a multi-party

* Tony Benn, 'Power, Parliament and People', *New Socialist*, Sept.–Oct. 1982.

contest for government and that is for political leaders themselves to guarantee such protection. They must develop conventions that will avoid placing the sovereign in a position where he or she has to make politically controversial decisions. It will not be easy for politicians to develop such conventions, and to observe them even when this runs counter to their party interest. For it will require them to acknowledge the existence of constitutional rules which take precedence over party conflict.

The Cabinet and the House of Commons

Proportional representation could also alter the role of the Cabinet and the House of Commons. A coalition Cabinet might work very differently from the single-party Cabinets to which Britain is mainly accustomed, for coalitions introduce an extra source of tension into Cabinet government. In addition to the normal political and departmental disagreements which occur in every administration, there would also be disputes between the parties concerning the allocation of ministerial posts and the implementation of the coalition programme. It would become more difficult for the Cabinet to operate as a unit and the Prime Minister might find it harder to assert his or her authority over recalcitrant Cabinet members.

Indeed, Prime Ministers would have to share power with other Ministers to a far greater extent than recent holders of that office have been willing to do. They would not be able to choose their Cabinets without consulting their coalition partners, nor would they retain the unfettered right to dismiss Ministers who incurred their displeasure. For, if they dismissed a Minister from the party of a coalition partner, this might be taken as an open challenge to the party concerned and therefore a threat to its participation in the coalition. If the dismissed Minister appealed to his or her party for support, there would be a breach in the coalition, and the solidarity of the Government would be at risk.

To avoid this extra source of friction in the working of

Cabinet government, decisions concerning the formation of the Government and the distribution of portfolios would have to be shared by the Prime Minister and the leader of the party with whom he or she is in coalition. The leader of the second party in the Government would be, in all but name, deputy Prime Minister, with a special role in Cabinet deliberations. His or her consent would be essential to the distribution of ministerial portfolios and to ministerial reshuffles. Policy, also, would have to be agreed between the parties comprising the coalition. Steering machinery might be developed for the purpose of ensuring that inter-party differences were resolved without rancour. Such machinery could not, of course, create agreement of itself. It is the will to reach agreement that would be vital, for above all, it would require a greater spirit of compromise to operate a coalition Government comprising two (or more) parties with independent power bases than a single-party Government.

One of the matters upon which the Government as a whole would have to agree is when to dissolve the coalition and appeal to the country. At present the decision as to when Parliament should be dissolved rests, by convention, with the Prime Minister, and it seems to have done so since 1918. It would be most unwise, however, for the second party in a coalition Government to allow the Prime Minister to retain this prerogative, for this would enable the Prime Minister to secure a tactical advantage over his or her coalition partners by threatening them with dissolution whenever agreement could not be reached. In a coalition, therefore, the decision to dissolve might well come to be taken by the Cabinet, as appears to have been the case before 1914.

Many advocates of proportional representation would seek to go further, arguing that the corollary of electoral reform must be fixed-term Parliaments, for the purpose of proportional representation is to ensure the sharing of power in government. But this purpose could always be circumvented if a Government, in danger of defeat in the Commons, decided to dissolve Parliament rather than seeking an accommodation with its critics. Fixed-term Parliaments would, on this view, block an escape route which could too easily be used by those who did not wish to seek agreement, for it would enable a Government, through the threat of dissolution, to put pressure on MPs who may be fearful of a general election.

This argument, however, takes a highly optimistic view of the possibilities of agreement in a multi-party context. It makes the assumption that an agreement can *always* be reached such as will allow a Government to be sustained until it comes to the end of its term. Yet if dissolution is impossible the result can easily be deadlock rather than agreement and a constructive compromise. To make dissolution more difficult would be to give a free licence to irresponsible parliamentary manoeuvring, and it would almost certainly damage the effectiveness of government. The possibility of dissolution should always be available to a Government as a last resort, even though, as we have seen, in a coalition the decision as to who should dissolve might well come to be made by the Cabinet rather than by the Prime Minister.

Indeed, a coalition, precisely because it implies the sharing of power, is likely to prove less susceptible to the display of prime ministerial power than a single-party Government. Some observers of British government have noticed a tendency in recent years towards prime ministerial government and believe that the Prime Minister's power *vis-à-vis* the Cabinet has gradually increased. Mrs Thatcher's Government is often cited as an example of this trend. Such dominance, however, would not be possible under a coalition. If there is prime ministerial government in Britain, it would be unlikely to survive the introduction of proportional representation and coalition government.

The relations between the Government and the Commons might also be changed by proportional representation. Many advocates of proportional representation hope that it would increase the power and authority of the Commons. The reasoning behind this view is that if there is no single-party majority in the Commons, the Government would have to rely upon the support of MPs from other parties. The Government, therefore, would have to take account of the views of backbenchers and would no longer be able to dismiss them as lobby fodder. Backbenchers would gain a real influence in the drafting and scrutiny of legislation, and Government Bills would rarely emerge unscathed from the Commons. Governments would cease to dominate the Commons; instead they would have to share power with MPs.

Such expectations, however, are probably utopian, for it is doubtful whether the introduction of proportional representation would in fact lead to a marked increase in backbench power. But the precise effects of proportional representation upon relations between Government and Parliament would depend upon which of the two systems, German or STV, was adopted.

Under the German system MPs could be even more beholden to their party than they are at present, for the party leadership would be able to demote a recalcitrant or rebel MP to a lower position on the party list, thus ensuring that he failed to secure re-election to the Commons. Under the British electoral system, on the other hand, a rebel MP can always retain his seat provided that he has the confidence of his constituency selection committee. The German system does involve the danger of giving excessive power to the party organization, thereby making the incentives to conform too great. It has been suggested by two critics of proportional representation that, under a system of the German type, Winston Churchill would not have been in the Commons in 1940. He would have been excluded by the party machine in 1935 for his opposition to the Baldwin Government.*

In the Federal German Republic party discipline is stricter than in Britain for this reason. It is quite rare for backbenchers to vote against their party's policies in Parliament. A member of the Bundestag is seen as very much a party delegate, whose

* Angus Maude and John Szemerey, *Why Electoral Change? The Case for Proportional Representation Examined* (London, Conservative Political Centre, 1982), p. 28.

duty it is to obey the decisions which the party has reached. It is difficult to be a party maverick under the German system.

Under STV, on the other hand, the power of the party machine would be less, since the MP would owe his seat not to nomination by the party organization but to the support of his constituents, who would have chosen him in preference to other members of his own party. Therefore the party leadership would have no means of ensuring that loyalists were returned to Parliament or dissidents defeated. An MP, provided that he maintained his constituency base, could defy his party with impunity. But it does not necessarily follow that MPs would use their independence to secure greater backbench influence over legislation in the House of Commons, for the dynamics of STV might well force them to devote themselves entirely to constituency work. That is certainly the case in Ireland, where the Dail is one of the weakest legislatures in Western Europe in terms of backbench influence on legislation, since its Members give far more time to constituency service than they do to matters of state. STV, therefore, could make MPs more parochial and less involved in policy issues than they are today. As David Butler has argued, 'The real cost of STV may lie in its effect on the behaviour of MPs. When every voter expresses a personal preference between candidates they may always be ousted by a more publicized member of their own party (or by the second preference of other parties). They will therefore have every incentive to labour the parish pump' (*The Times*, 23 July 1982). If that happened, MPs, although they would have gained independence from their party whips, would find themselves slaves to their constituents instead.

Such an outcome, however, is not inevitable, for under STV the type of MP chosen depends upon the voters. They may indeed choose MPs because of their qualities as constituency welfare officers: but, equally, they may decide to elect candidates who have something to contribute to the great issues of policy. The localist character of the Irish Dail may be a reflection more of the preferences of the Irish voter than of the intrinsic nature of STV. The British elector might well take a different view of the qualities needed in an MP. It is quite impossible to predict.

However, even if STV did lead to the return of more independent-minded MPs, eager to play an active role in the scrutiny of legislation and determined not to be influenced either by threats from the party Whips or offers of Government patronage, it is doubtful whether they would be able to display this independence when there was a coalition government. For a coalition relies for its survival upon a basis of mutual confidence between the various parties comprising it. This confidence depends upon observing agreements reached by the party leaders in Cabinet and elsewhere. Any revolt by backbenchers belonging to one of the parties in the coalition would appear as a breach of trust to members of the other party, or parties, in the government. Backbench dissent, therefore, even if it did not actually endanger the survival of the government, would threaten to undermine the mutual trust between coalition partners which would be essential if the Government was to be held together.

For this reason, a coalition Government might well need a greater degree of party discipline than is required by a single-party Government. In Germany, indeed, and in other Continental countries the formation of coalitions is made much easier precisely *because* the party list enables leaders to discipline recalcitrant members who are required to conform to coalition proposals.

In Britain, the only experience of coalition politics since the war, the 'Lib-Lab pact' of 1977–8, offers a good example of what can happen when party leaders are unable to enforce discipline. For the pact, in essence an agreement between the parliamentary Liberal Party and the Labour Cabinet, almost collapsed when it was found that the Cabinet could not commit Labour backbenchers to supporting legislation which the Liberals believed essential, such as the use of proportional representation in elections to the European Parliament. If this had been accepted by all Labour MPs, it would have gained a majority in the Commons. However, fewer than half the Labour MPs were willing to support it, and the proposal was defeated. This almost put a premature end to the pact because it destroyed the Liberals' belief in Labour's good faith, and it required all of David Steel's exertions to save the pact. Strains of this kind would be inevitable in a coalition Government unless backbenchers on each side of the coalition were willing to abstain from acting against their leaders' advice. Coalition, therefore, requires a high degree of party discipline. There is no reason to believe that it would undermine the Government's dominance of the House of Commons.

Coalition and Policy Outcomes

For anyone seeking to evaluate the merits and defects of proportional representation, the effects of a new electoral system upon Britain's political institutions are bound to be subordinate to the question of whether coalition is likely to lead to better government than single-party administrations have provided. In the past many people in Britain have seen coalitions, except in wartime or periods of economic emergency, as weak and unstable Governments, with the executive continually at the mercy of shifting party alignments in the legislature. The Weimar Republic in Germany, France before de Gaulle and contemporary Italy stand as warnings to this danger.

But coalition government need not necessarily be weak and unstable. For every example of such a coalition, it is possible to quote a counter-example of a country in which coalition provides stable, effective and accountable government. The most prominent examples of such coalitions are Germany and the Scandinavian countries. The truth is that the effectiveness of a Government is not fundamentally dependent upon either the existence of the absence of coalitions. The same range of policy outcomes is possible under coalitions as under single-party Governments. The important questions, therefore, are: under what conditions can coalition be expected to provide good government, and do these conditions obtain in contemporary Britain?

Where coalition government has worked badly – Germany in the 1920s, France before de Gaulle and contemporary Italy – politics has been conducted at a high ideological temperature, and there have been parties, such as the Nazis in Weimar Germany or the Poujadists in France in the 1950s, who were fundamentally opposed not just to the Government but to the political system itself. But in countries such as Sweden or contemporary Germany, where there is a basic consensus among the electorate, coalitions can be as stable and accountable as single-party Governments. Parties opposed to the system have so little support that they are unable to obtain more than a handful of seats in the legislature, if indeed they are able to secure representation at all; while the larger parties conduct their politics in a pragmatic and moderate way. Politics is marked by the peaceable adjustment of interests rather than a high rhetorical style.

Those who support proportional representation must, logically, welcome coalition, since this is a very likely consequence of a change in the electoral system. If they are to believe that coalition government is compatible with political stability, they must also take a particular view about British society. They must assume that British society is so fundamentally united that the basis for agreement between different parties is actually present. There would be sufficient common ground between the parties after proportional representation was introduced to make consensus possible. Opponents of proportional representation, on the other hand, claim that the very wide differences which exist between the parties in Britain today reflect a basic discord in society, and so there would be no agreement upon fundamentals even after the introduction of proportional representation.

What the supporters of electoral change constantly ignore [according to a recent Conservative Party policy pamphlet] is the existence of profound differences between political parties on fundamental issues – such as the control of public expenditure or the defence of the Falklands – which cannot be settled in 'smoke-filled rooms'. Instead of leading to an effective coalition on West German lines, a proportional representation election is more likely to produce a highly unstable minority Government (of the kind that existed in 1974–9) or total deadlock.*

It will be seen that any appraisal of the likely merits of coalition government, as of proportional representation itself, depends upon a view of the nature of society. Is British Society basically co-operative and consensual, or is it, rather, shot through with basic conflicts both extensive and profound. It is this question which lies at the very heart of the debate on proportional representation.

* Alistair B. Cooke, *Proportional Representation* (London, Conservative Research Department, 1983), p. 285.

8

Proportional Representation and the Condition of Britain

Multi-Party Politics

Proportional representation has come to the fore as an issue in British politics only in periods when the party system itself is in flux. At other times it has attracted little public attention, and for much of the twentieth century electoral change has not been a live issue. It has been the preserve solely of specialists in electoral matters, together with the Liberal Party, which since 1922, when it became the third party in British politics, has been officially committed to proportional representation. But it is only in two periods of the twentieth century – between 1906 and 1918, and since 1974 – that proportional representation has been able to excite the interest of the general public.

Between 1906 and 1918 proportional representation was a subject of real importance and concern in Britain. This was primarily a consequence of the rise of the Labour Party, since it seemed for a time as if Britain would remain a three-party system. Then, as now, political leaders were aware of the anomalies that would result from using an electoral system designed for only two parties; and Liberal and Labour leaders asked themselves how they could best avoid splitting the 'progressive' vote and allowing the Conservatives to win elections on a minority vote.

The First World War gave a further impetus to projects for

reform, for many believed that the post-war world would see the replacement of the two-party system by something new. The nation would face novel and unprecedented problems, whose solution would require a break with the methods of the past. In 1917 a Speakers Conference on electoral reform unamimously recommended that Britain adopt STV in urban constituencies and the alternative vote in rural constituencies. But this proposal was rejected by Parliament, ironically because Lloyd George, the Liberal leader, withheld his support from it, something which both he and the Liberal Party were to regret in the years that followed.

There was a brief flurry of interest in electoral reform during the years of the second minority Labour Government, from 1929 to 1931, but otherwise the subject lapsed as a topic of public concern until the general election of February 1974, which produced another hung Parliament and a minority Labour Government; while the gross under-representation of the Liberals who, despite gaining nearly one-fifth of the vote, won only 14 out of the 635 seats in the Commons, awakened many to the possible injustices of the British electoral system.

More recently, the birth of the SDP and the formation of the Liberal/SDP Alliance has brought the issue to the very forefront of the political stage because it has considerably strengthened the third force in British politics and hence made majority government less likely than it was before.

Indeed, the result of the 1983 general election means that the most likely alternative to a Conservative Government at the next election is no longer a Labour majority Government but a hung Parliament in which no single party enjoys an overall majority. For neither Labour nor the Alliance will enter an election in 1987 or 1988 in a strong enough position to win an overall majority on their own. For the first time since the 1920s there is no single-party alternative to the current administration.

Labour won 209 seats in the 1983 election and came second in 132. To win an overall majority in the Commons Labour would need to gain 117 seats, almost 90 per cent of the seats in which it came second. It would need a swing of well over 10 per cent to form a majority Government, a swing over twice as large as any that has been achieved in any general election since 1945.

The Alliance would need an even greater swing to gain an overall majority, for not only did it win around 2 per cent less of the vote than Labour in 1983 but also, as we have seen, it needs a larger percentage of the vote to gain an overall majority, since the distribution of its vote means that it will be under-represented in the Commons if it receives anything less than around 38 per cent of the vote.

It is questionable, then, to what extent the British electoral system is still capable, in a period of multi-party politics, of producing single-party Governments with overall majorities. It can certainly produce a Conservative Government with an overall majority, but the most likely alternative to a Conservative victory would be a hung Parliament, in which no party had a majority. In such a situation the Alliance would bargain hard to secure proportional representation, which it regards as a priority. Whether it will succeed in achieving a change in the electoral system must, however, be open to question, for the Alliance will come up against the self-interest of the Labour and Conservative parties, which cement their attachment to Britain's present electoral system.

Proportional Representation and the Party System

For party politicians, arguments about the merits and defects of proportional representation generally take second place to their estimate of what effect electoral change would have upon their party's fortunes. Since proportional representation would make it unlikely that either Labour or the Conservatives would be able to form a single-party Government without winning considerably more support than they can at present achieve, most Conservative and Labour leaders will resist change.

On occasion the professional politician's mask slips and the motivation behind the opposition to change is revealed. When, at the 1926 Labour Party Conference, Labour was considering whether or not to support proportional representation, one speaker claimed that it had worked in the interests of the capitalist parties. But from the platform George Lansbury, one of Labour's early leaders, argued that in the past he thought that the majority of the decisions under the present system had worked for the other people, but 'if they were wise, they could now make it work for themselves'. Ron Hayward, when General Secretary of the Labour Party, declared in 1977, 'Proportional representation means coalition government at Westminster, on the lines of our European partners, and it is goodbye then to any dreams of aspirations for a democratic socialist Britain', a revealing admission that such a 'democratic socialist Britain' could not be expected to command the support of a majority of the voters.

Leading Conservatives have been equally blatant in their defence of the British electoral system. At the Conservative Party Conference in 1975, Angus Maude rebutted the arguments for proportional representation by arguing:

> I believe that only the Conservatives, untrammelled and unhindered by the compromises of the left-centre, have the ability and the resolution to halt the slide of our economy and restore the citizen's faith in Parliament and in the future of British society. As far as I can see, no change in the electoral system will make it more likely that we would win or that we would govern, and most systems would make it less likely.

In other words, the essential test of an electoral system was whether it helped the Conservative Party win a general election, a test not perhaps likely to be accepted with much enthusiasm by the majority of voters who refused to vote Conservative in 1979 or 1983, nor, one suspects, by many Conservative supporters who may have a greater sense of fairness than their leaders.

It should not be thought that those who favour change in the electoral system necessarily do so from any purer motives. The

Liberal Party was hostile to proportional representation for as long as it was one of the major parties in the state. Gladstone claimed in 1884 that proportional representation was incomprehensible, while Joseph Chamberlain declared that opposition to proportional representation lay 'at the root of all Liberalism as I conceive it', since it was more 'dangerous to Liberal progress' than even 'the most overt Tory opposition'.* Asquith confessed that proportional representation was not a matter 'which excites my passions, and I am not sure that it even arouses any very ardent enthusiasm' (House of Commons, 4 July 1917), while Lloyd George thought it a device 'for bringing faddists of all kinds into Parliament' (House of Commons, 3 April 1917).† It was not until the Liberals became the third party in the system that they began to discover the merits of proportional representation.

There can be no doubt that party self-interest is the strongest factor determining the attitude of political leaders to proportional representation. That in itself is not reprehensible. Men and women would not enter politics unless they fervently believed in the principles and outlook of their party. It is only natural for them to favour arrangements which will assist their party to gain power and therefore to put their policies into effect, while resisting changes which would make it more difficult for their party to win a general election. What *is* reprehensible is that the decision about which electoral system is best for Britain should be made by politicians who have a vested interest in the existing system rather than by the electorate as a whole.

For the purpose of an electoral system is to register, as effectively as possible, the wishes of the voters in the election of the House of Commons and the formation of Governments. There are a number of possible ways of achieving this aim and no agreement on which is the best. Party leaders, however, are

---

* Letter to Sir John Lubbock, 14 October 1884, Lubbock Papers, British Library.
† Trevor Wilson (ed.), *The Political Diaries of C. P. Scott 1911–1928* (London, Collins, 1970), p. 274.

in the worst position to form a judgement on this issue, since the method adopted affects so much their prospects of gaining and losing power. The House of Commons may be the most suitable forum for pronouncing on the political decisions of the day. What is less certain is that it should also be able to pronounce on *how* decisions should be made. The constitution should belong to all and not merely to a temporary party majority.

On matters concerned with the boundaries of parliamentary constituencies and their amendment, Parliament has established a permanent body of Boundary Commissioners, which functions in a quasi-judicial way and operates independently of party. It is, perhaps, unrealistic to expect Parliament to adopt a similar method for recommending changes in the electoral system, but it ought not to be unrealistic to propose that Parliament should let the electorate decide, by means of referendum, whether the electoral system should be retained or changed. For the purpose of an election is not to serve the interests of *parties* but to ensure that the interests of *electors* are properly safeguarded, and the electors themselves are the most fitting judges of how this should be achieved. In a democracy sovereignty ought to belong to the electors, not to the parties.

Six Fallacies about Proportional Representation

If there were to be a referendum on proportional representation, should electors vote for change or for the status quo? Where does the balance of advantage lie? Discussion of the various alternative electoral systems in chapters 1 to 5 should make it possible to answer this question. But before attempting to reach a verdict, it is vital to clear away the fallacies about proportional representation which tend to dog discussion of the issue.

There is probably no political subject on which quite spurious arguments are heard with more frequency than proportional representation. One reason for this is the insularity which grips so many British commentators when discussing foreign countries; another is the complacent belief that Britain has little to learn from the experience of other countries, even though many European Governments have been able to combine democratic rule and economic progress with rather more success than their British counterparts have done.

Investigation of the German electoral system and the single transferable vote should have shown that many of the fears most commonly expressed about proportional representation are in reality quite groundless. It is worth listing the main fallacies which, it is hoped, earlier chapters of this book have exposed.

The first fallacy (and also the most foolish, although that does not prevent it from being frequently urged in debate) is that proportional representation is too complicated for the voter to understand. The premiss of this argument must be that the British voter is the most stupid in Europe. For every European country except Britain and France uses one or other of the various systems of proportional representation to elect its Parliament, and voters in these countries seem to have no difficulty at all in understanding how to use their vote intelligently. Further, STV – perhaps the most complex of the various proportional systems – was introduced into Northern Ireland at fairly short notice in 1973, and voters found no difficulty in using it. For a nation which enjoys the complexities involved in filling in football pools, neither the German electoral system nor STV would pose the slightest problem. To suggest otherwise is to insult the electorate.

The second fallacy is that proportional representation encourages political extremism and dictatorship. That is true of neither of the two systems discussed in this book, each of which operates in a well functioning democracy characterized by stable and moderate government. It is certainly the case that the democracies which Hitler and Mussolini demolished used proportional systems, but it is very doubtful whether these systems were responsible for the collapse of democracy in Germany and Italy. There were many far more fundamental weaknesses in the government and economy of those countries. It would be just as plausible to attack the British electoral system because its use in many African countries has been followed by the overthrow of democracy and the installation of authoritarian regimes. In any case, no one advocates that Britain should adopt the systems used by Germany or Italy in the 1920s.

The third fallacy is that proportional representation encourages the proliferation of parties, something which serves to undermine democratic accountability. Yet both Germany and the Irish Republic have seen a reduction in the number of parties under their proportional systems. Both systems employ mechanisms which prevent merely ephemeral 'flash' parties from disrupting the parliamentary system. To secure representation, parties must show that they are able to obtain a wide measure of support among a number of different groups. In West Germany and the Republic of Ireland there are *fewer* parties than there are in the Commons today.

The fourth fallacy is that proportional representation means frequent elections and rapid changes of government. Yet since 1960 only six countries have had more than one general election within a period of twelve months. Three of these, Ireland (1981–2), Greece (1963–4) and Portugal (1979–80), use proportional systems, while two, Britain (1974) and Canada (1979–80), use the British electoral system, and one, Japan (1979–80) uses a hybrid system which no one has suggested as suitable for Britain.* The average life of a Government in West Germany or the Irish Republic is the same as in Britain, and there is no evidence whatever that proportional representation is likely to lead to instability.

The fifth fallacy is that proportional representation, since it implies coalition government, deprives the elector of his right to choose a Government. This is true, as we have seen, neither in West Germany nor in the Republic of Ireland. In West Germany the voter can indicate his preference by splitting his

* David Butler, *Governing Without a Majority: Dilemmas for Hung Parliaments in Britain* (London, Collins, 1983), p. 69.

first and second votes, while in Ireland the pattern of inter-party transfers makes it almost impossible for the parties to ignore voters' wishes when it comes to the construction of coalitions. Nor do coalitions necessarily blur the account-ability of government. They serve to realign parties, not to eliminate opposition. In both Germany and Ireland, the voters are able to choose between coalition and single-party govern-ment. In Germany they have, in recent years, chosen coalition, while in Ireland the voters have generally, though by no means invariably, preferred single-party government. Where a party succeeds in convincing the majority of the voters of its case, it is almost always assured, under proportional representation, of winning a majority of seats in parliament and, as in Greece and Spain, both of which use proportional systems, coalition becomes unnecessary.

The sixth fallacy is that proportional representation neces-sarily destroys the link between MP and constituent. Whereas this may be true under some forms of proportional representa-tion, it is hardly applicable to the systems which have been discussed in this book. The German system retains the single-member constituency, while in Ireland the multi-member constituency and resulting competition between candidates means that electors are much better served by their MPs than voters in Britain today. Indeed, the main complaint against STV is that it is too localist. This amounts to saying that constituency representation would be so good under STV that other functions of the MP would come to be neglected. To claim that proportional representation would worsen rela-tionships between MPs and their constituents is, therefore, to ignore the truth as far as STV is concerned.

The Real Issues

When these fallacies have been cleared away, there remain the real issues to be considered. The case against the British electoral system is quite simply stated. It is that under the impact of three political groupings the system is likely to produce outcomes which increasingly fail to reflect the relationship between seats and votes. Such misrepresentation will serve to undermine the legitimacy, and therefore the effectiveness, of Parliament. It also makes the nation appear more divided than in fact it is. This is because the electoral system not only exaggerates the support of the leading party in the country as a whole, but it also over-represents the leading party in particular regions – the Conservatives in the south of England, Labour in the inner-city conurbations of the north. For this reason the parties come to seem less representative of the nation as a whole, and they find it difficult to surmount sectional and territorial interests.

What is at issue is not whether these anomalies exist – for few defenders of the British electoral system choose to deny them – but whether they are less tolerable than the disadvantages inherent in proportional systems. Supporters of proportional representation sometimes argue as if they believed that their favoured system entirely lacked faults, but there is no perfect electoral system, and any advocate of change has to weigh up and balance the various merits and defects of the different systems.

The analysis of the two main proportional systems has already revealed their central weaknesses. The German system can easily concede too much power to the party machine, while STV is not necessarily proportional, and it can produce perverse results, although in general it is likely to prove far more proportional than the British electoral system. But perhaps their greatest defect in the eyes of many is one which the two systems share – the excessive influence which they give to third parties (the Free Democrats in Germany or Labour in Ireland). Such parties, critics can argue, are able to win disproportionate influence if the major parties are unable to form a Government without their support.

In Britain proportional representation would put the Alliance in such a pivotal position. So although proportional representation would remove one form of unfairness, that suffered by parties which are under-represented in proportion to their vote, it would substitute for it another form of unfairness, giving the least popular of the three main political groupings too much influence over the formation of a Government. For proportional representation, although it ensures that each vote has (nearly) the same value, does not ensure that each party enjoys influence in proportion to its votes in the House of Commons. Parties of the centre which are willing to co-operate with parties of either left or right will exert more influence than non-co-operative or extremist parties. In Britain, therefore, it has been argued, 'Under the guise of giving fair representation, [PR] would actually have given to the smallest of the three parties the largest power to determine the nature of each Government.'*

It would, however, be wrong to imagine that a pivotal grouping such as the Alliance could exert this power in any way it chose. Its influence in negotiations would depend upon the extent to which its proposals were in accord with the wishes of its supporters and whether they were seen as responsible by the electorate as a whole. In previous periods when the Liberals have sustained minority Labour Governments – in 1924, 1929–31 and 1974 – they have found that this has led to a loss of electoral support; while their involvement with the Labour Government in 1977–8, under the terms of the 'Lib-Lab pact', also damaged the party electorally. A small party cannot hope to swing against the tide of public opinion and retain electoral credibility. It must, as the German Free Democrats have found, be particularly sure-footed and agile if it is to avoid being consigned to electoral oblivion. Many members of the Alliance, indeed, would probably prefer not to have to exercise this sort of responsibility; while some of the Alliance vote perhaps has the character of an inchoate protest against the two major parties, which would disappear when the Alliance was forced to take responsibility for political and governmental decisions. Critics

* Paper on proportional representation, 17 December 1935, CRD 1/72/1, Conservative Party Archives, Bodleian Library, quoted in Cooke, *Proportional Representation*, p. 285.

of proportional representation, therefore, exaggerate the power and room for manoeuvre which pivotal parties enjoy. It remains difficult to decide whether it is better to take the risk of allowing a pivotal party such influence in a system where it can be checked by a larger coalition partner, or whether it is better to allow the largest minority to govern, quite untrammelled by constitutional checks of any kind. That is a question that can be answered only by elaborating one's conception of democracy, for it touches on the very purpose of democratic institutions.

The Case for Proportional Representation

Attitudes to proportional representation tend to reflect radically different views of society and divergent conceptions of the democratic process. Those who favour proportional representation may be accused of taking a rather optimistic view of British society, which they believe to be fundamentally harmonious and fraternal. They do not deny the existence of conflict but believe that it is exaggerated by Britain's political institutions and especially the party system, which tends to the manufacture of conflict where none exists. Many advocates of proportional representation look longingly towards Scandinavia and West Germany, where conflict is contained in a political system which breeds conciliation and agreement. In such countries political stability is combined with social progress and efficient government. Supporters of proportional representation are said to make the optimistic assumption that if only the diverse interests in British society received fair representation, if only all the voices were heard, then consensus and agreement will be the result.

Opponents of proportional representation accuse reformers of being hopelessly idealistic. For them conflict is endemic in British society, and the party battle is but a reflection of real and substantial disagreeent between different social groups. Because such disagreement exists, the proportional representaiton of different interests in Parliament or Government will lead not to consensus and agreement but to immobilism. Nothing will be decided, and Britain will drift and stagnate, rather like Italy. Britain will become a country without government. For there is a genuine ideological division in Britain between advocates of a market economy and supporters of socialism, and it is for the electorate to choose between them. The only way in which Britain can be governed effectively, indeed governed at all, is by maintaining an electoral system which artificially creates a majority Government, ensuring that voters are presented with clear alternatives and forced to choose between competing priorities. Whatever its theoretical defects, therefore, the British electoral system provides the only method by which a divided society can be governed and strong decisions taken. Proportional representaiton, on the other hand, allows the electorate to avoid making choices, and so the country is prevented from following a clear path. It provides the worst of both worlds – consensus politics, the absence of clear direction and the sacrifice of all convictions in the interest of consensus.

Such would be the view not only of Margaret Thatcher but also of Neil Kinnock, Tony Benn and Enoch Powell, in agreement on this if on little else. It is the logical consequence of the Westminster model of government, but it is to take an essentially over-simplified view of politics to imagine that political alternatives can be confined to two ideologies – free-market liberalism and socialism – whose roots lie in the nineteenth century and which have little to offer in the way of solutions to the problems of a modern industrial society.

Advocates of proportional representation put forward a radical alternative to the Westminster model. They believe that democracy involves not the victory of one side over another in a battle fought between obsolete ideologies but a process of negotiation and agreement. The central strength of proportional representation is that it makes for the sharing of power at governmental level. This inculcates attitudes which spread outwards into society so that power in the economy and in industry also comes to be shared. Advocates of proportional representation tend to see it as a political concomitant, and indeed prerequisite, of power-sharing policies in the economic and social sphere – incomes policy, worker participation in industry and the restoration of a tripartite framework of co-operation between Government, industry and labour.

In no country [according to Sir Geoffrey Chandler, former Director General of the National Economic Development Office, in a lecture to the Royal Society of Arts in December 1982] was the pursuit of industrial consensus more needed: in none, for the very reasons that make it necessary would it have more difficulty in taking root. I stress *industrial* consensus because it is in the productive process that we have failed as a country. And by consensus I do not mean murky compromise or fudged policies: I mean the achievement of sufficient mutual understanding so that even without the unattainable goal of universal agreement, industrial decisions and policies will be based on a common analysis of the problem and, once made, can have a degree of consistency and continuity which will persist through different political administrations instead of suffering periodic reversal. It is a consensus implicitly perceived by managers and trade unionists through their common interest in continuity and stability, but has been inordinately damaged by the pendulum of party politics pulling against this underlying convergence.

Conflict in British society can be resolved only through the construction of mechanisms of consensus, however painful that process may be. But its rewards are very great; for the economic and social record of countries which adhere to the power-sharing model of government is far superior to that of countries such as Britain, clinging to an adversary conception of politics which is far too crude to cope with the complexities of modern industrial society. Advocates of proportional representation wish to see adversary politics replaced by the politics of mutual accommodation, without which no industrial society can be governed successfully in the political conditions of the late twentieth century.

The fundamental argument for proportional representation, therefore, is not only that it will remove the distortions inevitable when three political groupings compete within an electoral system designed for two, but also that it will enable government to be conducted more in accord with modern conditions. Either of the two main systems discussed in this book, the German system or STV, would ensure that Governments reflected the opinions of voters more accurately than the British electoral system allows. But STV would allow greater popular participation in politics and therefore greater identification with government. It would give almost every voter a direct stake in the election of his or her local MP and provide a choice going beyond that of party nominees. For this reason it would have an educative effect upon voters, encouraging them to think of political issues in other than simplistic party terms. Governments would be forced to take a wider range of opinion into account before formulating their policies, and this would encourage the growth of a spirit of accommodation which is likely to extend into the industrial sphere and into wider social relationships. STV, therefore, is the electoral system which is most likely to refashion the processes of British government, so that they can more suitably meet the complex problems of a society which can be governed successfully only if due regard is had to the susceptibilities of all of its members.

But will proportional representation militate against strong government? 'Strong government' is a term whose meaning is rarely made entirely clear. In Britain 'strong government' is equated with the enjoyment of an overall majority in the House of Commons. But in a democracy can government be strong if the majority does not want it? The British electoral system positively misleads Governments about the extent of their popular support and encourages them to believe that they enjoy a mandate for measures which are favoured by only a minority of the electorate. Governments become only too ready to neglect the search for agreement which constitutes the very essence of politics in a modern democracy. 'No Government,' declared Winston Churchill, 'which is in a large minority in the country, even though it possess a working majority in the House of Commons, can have the necessary power to cope with real problems' (House of Commons, 2 June 1931). Strong government is more likely to be the product of an administration which enjoys majority support in the country, rather than of one whose support in the Commons is artificially exaggerated by the electoral system. In a modern democracy the only strong government worthy of the name is one that can mobilize the consent of the electorate behind its policies. Viewed in these terms, the British electoral system produces neither strong government nor good government. It has also come seriously to offend against fundamental democratic principles.

To meet the canons of democracy, an electoral system should perform two functions. It should ensure, first, that the majority rules and, secondly, that all significant minorities are heard. It is because the British electoral system now violates both conditions that the case for reform of the electoral system is likely to be pressed with increasing insistence in the years to come.

Suggestions for Further Reading

The basic account of the working of the British electoral system is David Butler, *The British Electoral System since 1918*, 2nd edn (Oxford, OUP, 1963). David Butler has also written, with Dennis Kavanagh, the standard work, *The British General Election of 1983* (London, Macmillan, 1984). There is also a highly technical account of why the British electoral system works so badly in a three-party system by Graham Gudgin and P. J. Taylor, *Seats, Votes and the Spatial Organisation of Elections* (London Pion, 1979).

On the German electoral system, Tony Burkett, *Parties and Elections in West Germany: The Search for Stability* (London, Hurst, 1975), is thoroughly reliable. Apparently a new edition of this work is being prepared.

Cornelius O'Leary, *Irish Elections, 1918–1977: Parties, Voters and Proportional Representation* (Dublin, Gill and Macmillan, 1979), provides a balanced overview of the working of the Irish system over a period of 60 years; while the November 1982 election can be followed in detail from either *Nealon's Guide to the 24th Dail and Seanad* (Dublin, Platform Press, 1983), or Magill *Book of Irish Politics 1983* (Dublin, Magill, 1983).

Elizabeth Vallance, *Women in the House* (London, Athlone Press, 1979) shows how proportional representation would assist with the election of women to the House of Commons; John Curtice's pamphlet, *Proportional Representation and Britain's Ethnic Minorities* (Centre for Contemporary Studies,

1983) does the same for Britain's black and Asian communities.

Vernon Bogdanor (ed.), *Coalition Government in Western Europe* (London, Heinemann, 1983), contains essays on the working of coalitions on the Continent; David Butler, *Governing Without a Majority: Dilemmas for Hung Parliaments in Britain* (London, Collins, 1983), and Part 2 of Vernon Bogdanor, *Multi-Party Politics and the Constitution* (Cambridge, CUP, 1983), discuss the likely constitutional consequences of Parliaments in which no single party enjoys an overall majority; while Tony Benn, 'Power, Parliament and People', in the Labour Party journal, *New Socialist*, Sept.–Oct. 1982, is a characteristically provocative contribution to the debate.

There is a large literature arguing the case for proportional representation but comparatively little putting the opposite viewpoint. Of books in the former category, Enid Lakeman, *Power to Elect: The Case for Proportional Representation* (London, Heinemann, 1982), can be thoroughly recommended as a reliable and lively tract; while S. E. Finer (ed.), *Adversary Politics and Electoral Reform* (London, Anthony Wigram, 1975), has exerted considerable influence on the subsequent debate.

The best scholarly treatment of the case against proportional representation is to be found in chapter 12 of Philip Norton's *The Constitution in Flux* (Oxford, Martin Robertson, 1982). Otherwise, the reader who seeks to investigate this viewpoint is confined largely to literature produced by the political parties. Much of this is disfigured by factual inaccuracies and unsupported generalizations, but an exception is Alistair B. Cooke, *Proportional Representation*, Politics Today Series, No. 15 (1983), produced by the Conservative Research Department.

There are two organizations dedicated to pursuing the case for proportional representation, and each of them publishes a good deal of valuable literature on the subject. They are the National Committee for Electoral Reform, 60 Chandos Place,

London WC2, and the Electoral Reform Society, 6 Chancel Street, Southwark, London SE1, which argues for the single transferable vote.

A history of the debate about proportional representation in Britain can be found in Parts 3 and 4 of Vernon Bogdanor, *The People and the Party System* (Cambridge, CUP, 1981).

Index

Adams, Gerry, 121–2
additional members, 70, 71, 72
Alliance, Liberal/SDP, 5, 16, 17, 18, 19, 20, 21, 22, 23, 24, 25, 27, 36, 37, 39, 42, 61, 70, 71, 76, 77, 78, 94, 96, 100, 101, 119, 120, 129, 130, 131, 143, 144, 151, 152
Andrae, Carl, 75
Asquith, H. H., 128, 146
Australia, 31, 34, 41, 43, 77
Australian Labour Party, 41, 43
Australian Liberal Party, 41, 43

Baldwin, Stanley, 136
Belgium, 26, 114
Benn, Tony, 132, 154
best losers, 70–3
Brandt, Willy, 52, 56
by-elections, 52, 97

Cabinet government, 133–5
Callaghan, James, 8, 9, 13, 61
Chamberlain, Joseph, 146
Chandler, Sir Geoffrey, 155
Chitnis, Lord, 112
Christian Democrats, German (CDU/CSU), 10, 11, 12, 50, 51, 52, 53, 54, 55, 56, 59, 60, 61, 62, 63, 64, 65, 66, 67, 94, 129

Churchill, Winston, 128, 136, 157
coalition government, 8, 41, 53, 59, 60, 61, 62, 63, 64, 65, 66, 73, 74, 80, 81, 93, 94, 95, 99, 100, 107, 108, 109, 128, 129, 130, 131, 133, 134, 135, 138–9, 140–1, 145, 149, 150, 153
collective Cabinet responsibility, 109
consensus politics, 19, 67, 68, 140, 141, 153, 154, 155, 156, 157
Conservative Party and Government, 5, 8, 9, 10, 14, 15, 16, 17, 18, 19, 21, 22, 23, 24, 25, 27, 28, 32, 34, 35, 36, 38, 39, 42, 43, 44, 55, 58, 59, 68, 70, 71, 77, 78, 80, 101, 102, 103, 118, 119, 128, 130, 131, 140, 142, 143, 144, 151
De Valera, Eamon, 80, 81, 107
Denmark, 75, 76, 114
Fianna Fail, 79, 80, 81, 84, 87, 89, 91, 92, 94, 95, 97, 98, 99, 106, 108, 109, 130
Fine Gael, 79, 80, 81, 87, 89, 91, 92, 93, 95, 97, 98, 99, 108, 130

FitzGerald, Garret, 80, 130
France, 31, 37, 46, 139, 140
Free Democrats, German (FDP),
 10, 11, 12, 50, 51, 52, 53, 54,
 55, 56, 59, 60, 61, 62, 63, 64,
 65, 66, 67, 71, 94, 129, 130,
 151, 152

general elections:
 Australia (1977), 41
 Britain (1945), 43; (1951), 14,
  16, 19; (1964), 41; (1966),
  42, 43; (1970), 42, 124;
  (February 1974), 14, 15,
  16, 20, 23, 24, 32, 61, 124,
  128, 130; (October 1974),
  15, 16, 20, 23, 31, 32, 34,
  41, 61, 124, 128, 130,
  143; (1979), 9, 14, 16, 23,
  27, 42, 43, 54, 61, 128,
  130; (1983), 1, 3, 14, 16,
  20, 21, 22, 23, 24, 25, 26,
  27, 31, 32, 36, 42, 43, 54,
  55, 61, 100, 124, 125,
  130, 143)
 France (1981), 42
 Germany (1965), 65; (1969),
  60, 61, 65, 66; (1972), 54,
  60, 61, 66; (1976), 10, 11,
  54, 60, 61; (1980), 10, 11,
  54; (1983), 51, 53, 54, 55,
  60, 61, 62, 66, 129
 Ireland (1965), 98, 99;
  (1969), 98, 99; (1973), 93,
  98, 99; (November 1982),
  79, 80, 81, 93, 97, 102,
  117, 129, 130
 South Africa (1948), 44–5
German electoral system, 10, 30,
 ch. 4 *passim*, 94, 97, 102,
 111, 113, 115, 116, 118,
 120, 121, 124, 125, 126,
 136–7, 148, 149, 150, 151,
 153, 156

Germany, Federal Republic, 10,
 ch. 4 *passim*, 114, 115, 116,
 121, 122, 123, 124, 129,
 136, 138, 139, 140, 148,
 149, 150
Gladstone, W. E., 146
Glasgow, 15, 27, 28, 44, 72,
Grand Coalition (Germany), 60,
 61, 62, 66
Greens (Germany), 51, 52, 53,
 54, 55, 56

Hailsham, Lord, 24
Hare, Thomas, 75
Haughey, Charles, 81, 92, 93,
 130
Hayward Ron, 145,
Heath, Edward, 15
Heseltine, Michael, 28
Hill, Sir Rowland, 75
Hill, Thomas Wright, 75, 78
Hitler, Adolf, 48, 59, 122, 123,
 148
House of Commons, 135–9

inner cities, 28, 101, 102, 118,
 151
Ireland, Republic of, 47, 48, ch.
 5 *passim*, 113, 114, 117,
 121, 122, 129, 137, 149, 150
Irish Labour Party, 79, 80, 81,
 87, 89, 90, 91, 92, 93, 95, 97,
 98, 99, 108, 151
Italy, 48, 113, 114, 122, 123,
 124, 139, 140, 148, 149, 154

Kohl, Helmut, 11, 12, 63, 66

Labour Party and Government,
 5, 9, 10, 14, 15, 16, 17, 18,
 19, 21, 22, 23, 24, 25, 26, 27,
 28, 32, 34, 35, 36, 38, 39, 42,
 43, 55, 59, 61, 68, 70, 71, 77,
 78, 79, 80, 96, 101, 102,

103, 108, 118, 119, 128, 129, 130, 131, 138–9, 142, 143, 144, 145, 151, 152
Lansbury, George, 145
'Lib–Lab pact', 9, 61, 138, 152
Liberal Party, 9, 11, 12, 13, 16, 17, 18, 19, 25, 32, 34, 35, 37, 38, 39, 40, 58, 59, 61, 76, 77, 94, 128, 130, 138, 139, 142, 143, 146, 152
Liverpool, 15, 27, 28, 101, 102
Lloyd George, David, 76, 128, 143, 144

majority government, 4, 15, 16, 59, 129, 143, 144, 154, 157
Malta, 76, 77, 97, 98, 109, 114, 117
Maltese Labour Party, 97, 98
Maude, Angus, 145
Mill, J. S., 75
minority government, 8, 9, 16, 41, 128, 129, 141, 143
minority vote, 31, 32, 37, 39, 40, 43, 44, 45, 73, 142
Mintoff, Dom, 97
Morley, John, 121
multi-member constituencies, 41, 78, 79, 81, 84, 90, 94, 96, 100, 101, 103, 104, 105, 106, 108, 113, 117, 119, 120, 125, 150, 152
Mussolini, Benito, 122, 123, 124, 148

National Country Party (Australia), 41, 43
National Front, 73, 121–6
Nationalists (Malta), 97, 98
Nazi Party, 122, 123, 140
Netherlands, 114, 115
Northern Ireland, 47, 55, 56, 76, 81, 86, 88, 89, 148

party list, 40, 52, 56, 57, 58, 64, 68, 69, 70, 71, 73, 74, 103, 113, 114, 115, 116, 117, 119, 136, 138
Pitt, Lord, 112, 118, 119, 120
pivot party, 60, 61, 62, 130, 131, 151–2, 153
Plaid Cymru, 17, 55, 56, 101
primary elections, 57, 58, 90, 91, 102

quota, electoral, 84, 85, 86, 87, 88, 96, 120, 125

Scandinavia, 114, 115, 124, 139, 153
Scheel, Walter, 56
Schmidt, Helmut, 11, 12, 13, 52, 63
Scottish National Party (SNP), 17, 32, 34, 35, 36, 38, 55, 56, 70, 71, 101
senatorial rules, 86
single-member constituencies, 40, 53, 56, 69, 72, 102, 103, 105, 108, 113, 114, 115, 116, 117, 150
single-party government, 15, 109, 128, 129, 133, 135, 139, 140, 144, 150
Single transferable vote (STV), 31, 47, 48, ch. 5 *passim*, 111, 117, 118, 120, 121, 122, 124, 125, 126, 136–8, 143, 148, 149, 150, 151, 156
Sinn Fein, 121–2
Social Democratic Party (SDP), Britain, 16, 19, 39, 40, 55, 61, 76, 94, 108, 143
Social Democrats (SPD), Federal Republic of Germany, 10, 11, 12, 51, 52, 53, 54, 55, 56, 59, 60, 61, 62, 63, 64, 65, 66, 67

Speaker's Conference, 75, 143
split vote, *see* minority vote
stable government, 47, 48, 106, 107, 122, 124, 148, 149
Steel, David, 139
Strauss, Franz Josef, 12, 67
surplus, transfer of under STV, 85–8
Sweden, 114, 115, 140

Tactical voting, 39, 40
Thatcher, Margaret, 4, 8, 9, 24, 25, 68, 105, 135, 154
three-party system, 19–26, 99, 130, 132, 150–1, 156
threshold, 50, 51, 54, 55, 56, 59, 63, 64, 70, 73, 97, 99, 124, 125
two-party system, 5, 18, 19, 20, 26, 99, 143
turnout, 54, 106

Ulster Unionists, 17
United States of America, 57, 90, 113, 114, 120

wasted votes, 44, 55, 77, 78, 89, 90
Weimar Republic, 48, 50, 122, 123, 124, 139, 140
Westminster model, 109, 154
Workers Party (Irish Republic), 90, 93, 97, 108